Selected Lyric Poetry

NORTHWESTERN WORLD CLASSICS

*Northwestern World Classics brings readers
the world's greatest literature. The series features
essential new editions of well-known works,
lesser-known books that merit reconsideration,
and lost classics of fiction, drama, and poetry.
Insightful commentary and compelling new translations
help readers discover the joy of outstanding writing
from all regions of the world.*

Alexander Pushkin

Selected Lyric Poetry

Translated from the Russian and
annotated by James E. Falen

Northwestern University Press ✦ *Evanston, Illinois*

Northwestern University Press
www.nupress.northwestern.edu

Printed in the United States of America
10   9   8   7   6   5   4   3   2   1

Library of Congress Cataloging-in-Publication Data

Pushkin, Aleksandr Sergeevich, 1799–1837.
    [Poems. English. Selections]
    Selected lyric poetry / Alexander Pushkin ; translated from the
Russian and annotated by James E. Falen.
        p. cm. — (Northwestern world classics)
ISBN 978-0-8101-2642-8 (pbk. : alk. paper)
    1. Pushkin, Aleksandr Sergeevich, 1799–1837—Translations into
English. I. Falen, James E., 1935– II. Title. III. Series: Northwestern
world classics.
PG3347.A2F36 2009
891.713—dc22

                                                                2009019636

Lyrics 1830–1837

Alexander Sergeevich Pushkin (1799–1837) is the writer whom Russians regard as both the source and the summit of their literature, their greatest poet and their national pride. A few words on his life and his legacy are an appropriate introduction to this selection of his lyrics.

Even as a schoolboy Pushkin demonstrated a precocious talent for verse, and he was early recognized as a poetic prodigy by prominent older writers. In 1817 he received a nominal appointment in the government service, but for the most part he led a dissipated life in the capital while he continued to produce much highly polished light verse. His narrative poem *Ruslan and Liudmila* (published in 1820) brought him widespread fame and secured his place as the leading figure in Russian poetry. At about the same time a few mildly seditious verses led to his banishment from the capital. During this so-called southern exile, he composed several narrative poems and began his novel in verse, *Eugene Onegin*. Further conflicts with state authorities, however, soon led to a new period of exile at his family's estate of Mikhailovskoye. There he wrote some of his finest lyric poetry, completed his verse drama *Boris Godunov*, and continued work on *Eugene Onegin*. He was still in enforced absence from the capital when the Decembrist revolt of 1825 took place. Although several of his friends were among those executed or imprisoned, he himself was not implicated in the affair, and in 1826 he was pardoned by the new Czar Nicholas I and permitted to return to Moscow. By the end of the decade, as he sought to become a truly professional writer, he turned increasingly to prose composition. In the especially fruitful autumn of 1830, while stranded by cholera at his estate of Boldino, he completed *Eugene Onegin*, wrote a major collection of prose stories (*The Tales of Belkin*), and composed his experimental *Little Tragedies.* In 1831 he married Natalya Goncharova and sought to put his personal and professional affairs on a more stable footing. The rest of his life, however, was plagued by financial and marital woes, by the hostility of literary and political enemies, and by the younger generation's dismissal of his recent work. His literary productivity diminished, but in the remarkable "second Boldino autumn" of 1833 he produced both his greatest prose tale, *The Queen of Spades,* and a last poetic masterpiece, *The Bronze Horseman.* In 1836 he completed his only novel-length work in prose, *The Captain's Daughter.* Beleaguered by numerous adversaries and enraged by anonymous letters containing attacks on his honor, he was driven in 1837 to challenge an importunate admirer of his wife to a duel. The contest took place on January 27, and two days later the poet died from his wounds.

Within the Russian tradition the scope of Pushkin's achievement is clear and well established. He is unarguably a figure of protean dimensions, the author in his own right of a formidable and enduring body of work and at the same time the seminal writer whose example has nourished, enriched, and in large part directed much of the subsequent literature in the language. He came of age at a historical moment when the Russian literary language, after a century or so of imitation of foreign models, had been roughly shaped and readied for the hand of an original genius. Pushkin fulfilled that role.

He began his career in an era when both the writers and the readers of literature belonged almost exclusively to the limited milieu of aristocratic society and at a time when poetry rather than prose was the dominant mode for high literature. Well-read in both the ancient classics and in Western European literature, especially French literature of the seventeenth and eighteenth centuries, Pushkin was the most dazzlingly talented member of a younger generation of writers who were attempting, under the banner of romanticism, to reform and invigorate the language and styles of poetry. If Pushkin's early work was facile and conventional, consisting mainly of light verse suitable for the literary salons of the day (frothy epicurean pieces, witty epigrams, album verse), it already displayed an impressive plasticity of language that was new in Russian literature; and quite soon he exhibited a mastery of virtually all the poetic genres and styles known to the writers of his era. The eventual range of his creativity was enormous, embracing not only all the prevailing forms of lyric verse (which he reshaped into his own freer medium of expression), but including brilliant examples of narrative verse as well. He also achieved stunning success in poetry based on the idioms and themes of Russian folklore, and he experimented fascinatingly in the field of verse drama, both on a large Shakespearian scale and in intensely concentrated, minimalist studies of human passions. Possessed of a uniquely supple linguistic instrument, he is the master of an apparently effortless naturalness, a seamless blend of appropriate sound, sense, and feeling. During the last decade of his life, Pushkin turned increasingly to prose and showed himself a master here as well, with a style characterized by an unusual terseness and precision of expression. He also made significant contributions to Russian culture as a literary critic and editor, as an accomplished letter writer, and as a gifted, if amateur, historian. He is, in sum, a writer of astonishing versatility and Russia's first complete man of letters.

All his creative life Pushkin suffered from the indignities and impositions of an autocratic state: exile in his youth, the frustrations of police surveillance and a grossly interfering censorship in his later years, the constant and onerous obligations of state service, and the continuing humiliation of having to rely on imperial favor. In an effort to secure his independence from such state control over his affairs, he gave his allegiance to a kind of "aristocratic party," seeing in the old Russian landed gentry, the class to which he himself belonged, the only viable check on the arbitrary power of the autocracy.

In both his poetry and his prose, Pushkin was a profound innovator. He brought to its successful conclusion the revolt against the tenets of French neoclassicism, which, with its rigid divisions and classifications of genres, had dominated the literature of the eighteenth and early nineteenth centuries. Life, in Pushkin's view, was wilder and more various than these conventions would allow, and although he always retained a rather classical respect for balance and proportion in art, he introduced into his native literature a new sense of artistic freedom. His formal experiments encouraged a vigorous inventiveness in the writers who followed him, and his modernization of the diction and syntax of literary texts with infusions of living contemporary speech pointed the way to a perennial renewal of the literary language. In the area of literary subject matter as well, his influence was far-reaching: he introduced a host of suggestive themes that later writers would explore more fully, and he greatly enlarged the cast of characters in serious literature. He virtually created and shaped modern Russian literature and in countless ways determined the course it would follow after him.

Those who seek labels have made numerous attempts to define and categorize this astonishing writer. He has been called variously a romantic and a realist, the poet of freedom, and the bard of Russia's imperium; he has been dubbed in political terms a radical, a liberal, and a conservative; and he has been considered a revolutionary critic of the czarist regime and its loyal defender. Persuasive arguments can be made in support of each of these characterizations, but a poet of genius always in the end evades our efforts to tame and contain him.

This brief assessment of Pushkin's place in Russian literature, although it provides a reasonably accurate recital of established critical views, ignores certain anomalies and paradoxes that are part of the Pushkin story. Rather curiously, for example, all the prolific and prodigious achievement of this "father of Russian literature" was the work of a man whose chief public mask in his own day was that of a gadfly and wastrel. Disciplined in his art, he was often irresponsible and profligate in his social behavior. There was about him, as the reminiscences of contemporaries observe, something of the eternal schoolboy and prankster, a bit of the renegade always at odds with the respectable adult world. For several years he played the roles of dandy or bohemian; he loved to shock with outlandish dress or outrageous behavior, and he enjoyed flirting recklessly with the dangers of a dissident and dissolute life. Upon leaving school, he put on, briefly, the mask of political rebel and quite consciously provoked, with several courageous poems of liberal sentiment, the displeasure of the emperor, for which he was punished with removal from the centers of Russian culture and power. Even then, in banishment, he courted further punitive action from the authorities by circulating verse of blasphemous, if humorous, content.

Exile seems to have been a defining experience of Pushkin's young manhood. He deeply resented his enforced absence from the social scene, yet he gained through his distance from the center of events a clearer vision of the society he craved to rejoin. When he was permitted, eventually, to reside once again in St. Petersburg and Moscow, he quickly set about to re-establish his nonconformist credentials, indulging once more in a dissipated style of life, although it now seemed less appropriate to his advancing years. Even after his marriage (at almost 32 years of age), when he had ostensibly settled down, he continued to provoke outrage, antagonism, and even ridicule with his endless literary feuds, his increasingly touchy pride in his ancient lineage, and his contempt for the circles of the court. Yet another cause for the contradictory impulses of his spirit was the black African strain in his ancestry, a heritage that he saw as both a source of uniqueness and a mark of his alienation from the society whose acceptance he simultaneously rejected and craved. At times he reveled in his "African strangeness" and spoke of his "Moorish" features as the emblem of an elemental and primordial side of his identity, while on other occasions he lamented the racial characteristics that set him apart from those around him. All in all, it seems clear that Pushkin relished as well as resented his estrangement from society; and certainly his marginal position in it helped him to see all the triviality and hypocrisy of the *monde*. If he continued to live by its codes, he also studied it keenly as an artist and depicted it matchlessly in his work.

Even by the standards of his time and circle, Pushkin's appetite for dissipation was large. He was an inveterate gambler and a famous seducer of women, behavior that he was reluctant to relinquish not merely out of a mindless adherence to fashionable social roles but because of the special powers that he attributed to chance and sensuality in his creative life. His youthful Anacreontic verse with its playful eroticism, several narrative poems of refined ribaldry, and his more mature love poetry all testify to a deeply sensual nature; and his passion for gambling figures prominently in some of his finest prose works. He was always fascinated, on behalf of his art, in the play of the fortuitous, in the luck of the draw, in the creative possibilities of life's contingencies. He was willing as man and artist to trust in chance, to submit to it as the mechanism that, although it might condemn him to an outwardly undefined and precarious existence, would also assure his inner artistic freedom and his poetic destiny. Chance, in Pushkin's view, was the servant of the greater thing that he called Fate, and his reverence for fate as the ultimate shaper of human destinies haunts his work at almost every stage of his career. Essentially buoyant and optimistic in his youth, perceiving fate as the artist's benign and essential guide, he would never distrust it, not even when later in his life it took on an ominous and threatening aspect. Opposition to the tyranny of human institutions was an essential element in Pushkin's conception of the free artist, but resistance to fate, he believed, was a perilous course of action for any individual; for himself, he was convinced, it was the surest way to destruction as a poet. These features of Pushkin's character—his sensuality, his courting of chance, and his trust in fate—are defining clues to his artistic being and to his conception of creativity. He is an artist for whom the private personality stands for little, for whom an ordinary human nature and a mundane existence are the very attributes and signs of the poet who is fully engaged with life and at the same time receptive to the designs of Providence.

The poet for Pushkin is a mysterious being: the instrument and voice of powers beyond the self; and yet he remains at an everyday level the most ordinary of humans, at times even a misfit and outcast. This is a conception of the poet that combines elements of both a romantic and an antiromantic sensibility. It yokes together two disparate images, that of the divinely inspired seer and that of the human pariah. It is a vision, of course, with ancient roots and, in its specifically Russian context, with links to the native tradition of the *iurodivy,* the wandering "holy fool" of popular veneration. For Pushkin such an image of the poet provides a justification for asserting at once an enormous arrogance for his art and a fundamental humility toward himself. And perhaps it helps to explain the peculiar instability of his artistic personality, the odd sense his reader has that, despite a powerful presence in his work, the writer himself remains enigmatic and elusive. His genius is to an unusual extent of a peculiarly negative kind. He is that rare artist who possesses to an extreme degree a kind of splendid receptivity, an ability to absorb and embody the very energy of his surroundings, to take into himself with an amazing sympathy all the shapes and colors of the life he sees and hears and to which he responds. His calling as an artist is to re-create that life in all its vivacity and variety, to display his sheer perception of it, refraining from an easy human judgment.

Pushkin is something of an artistic chameleon, which is why it is so difficult to define him or to fix on a clear and consistent image of his authorial person and stance. He seems, at times, almost to lack a coherent artistic persona; like a chameleon, he seems capable of changing his colors and of adapting to virtually any milieu. Enormously alive to the ephemera of experience, he is fascinated by everything and everyone: the sublime and the ridiculous, the sacred and the profane, and all the roles that people play and every style of behavior. He is interested equally in the talented and the mediocre, in the articulate and the dumb, in czars, peasants, soldiers, fops, rakes, society women, vulnerable girls, rascals, villains, and almost everyone else. He wants, if only fleetingly, to capture everything, to absorb it all in his appetite for life—even at the risk of losing himself, or perhaps out of the need to lose himself. And this restless curiosity lends a kind of lightness as well as universality to his work—a lightness of touch, weight, and illumination. The quality is legendary in descriptions of Pushkin's art, but it can be mistaken for superficiality. This elusive author appears to take few things seriously (not excluding himself) and he often poses as a mere entertainer. Entertaining he certainly is, but if we, as readers, are taken in by his ruse and allow ourselves to become inattentive, we are in danger of missing the subtle and hidden aspects of his art.

The effect of lightness, the exceptional clarity that so famously accompanies Pushkin's breadth of interests, goes hand in hand with his vaunted terseness and simplicity, his evident and easy accessibility. But his terseness can be more apparent than real, for his art has the capacity to suggest much in a few spare and simple observations; and his simplicity can be deceptive, screening from the casual reader an art of great sophistication and delicacy. To the foreign reader, especially, Pushkin's qualities of clarity and simplicity can be an impediment to the appreciation of his work; and if the reader has first come to Russian literature through the tormented and profound explorations of Tolstoy or Dostoevsky, Pushkin's view of the passing scene, filled with a bracing humor as well as grief, may produce a rather strange impression. He is not at all what such a reader has come to expect of a Russian writer. Unlike those two later masters, Pushkin is not in any overt way either a philosopher or a religious thinker, not a didactic moralist or an analytic psychologist. He is both more universal in his sympathies and more modest in his artistic persona.

Perhaps, in his final years, this poet of light could not fully adjust to the passing of his youth and the waning of youth's poetic energy. If he would not become a poet of the dark, perhaps he did in the end become the seer of an "unbearable lightness of being." In several of his later poems some spectral beast of retribution seems to haunt the poet's mind, along with premonitions of, and even yearnings for, an early death. But the ending in human life is always the same, whereas in great art, as in the plenitude of Pushkin's work, it can at least seem otherwise. Pushkin retained to the last his humility before Providence and he went to his duel and his death completely in character. We cannot, finally, explain the creative power of this extraordinary writer; we can only say with some degree of certainty that he is Russia's most complete artist, its closest thing to the pure poet incarnate, that being who sacrifices all the other possibilities of human existence to the expression, through language, of life's fascinating variety. The aim of poetry, Pushkin asserted, is poetry itself. The poet emerges from the creative spirit to show us the world and speak of things beyond our normal ken; he is the voice of time's fleeting and intricate fullness.

Several years ago, after I had finished my translation of Push-kin's *Eugene Onegin: A Novel in Verse* (Oxford University Press, World Classics Series), I felt educated and emboldened enough to try translating some of the lyric poetry by Russia's greatest poet. The selection of verse offered here is the result of that effort. Some of these translations have appeared previously in various scholarly journals and collections; others are given here for the first time.

I have arranged the lyrics more or less chronologically, beginning with verse written in the poet's teenage years and closing with lines composed shortly before his death. Included are many famous poems, well known to every educated Russian (often by heart), as well as lighter, more occasional pieces. I have adhered for the most part in these English versions to Pushkin's own formal poetic structures, to the patterns of his meter and rhyme. At times, however, I have replaced feminine rhymes with masculine ones (placing the stress, that is, on the final rather than the penultimate syllables). This has seemed to me a reasonable decision, since in most English poetry the masculine rhyme prevails, its pride of place sanctioned and sanctified by the language's great tradition. In Shakespeare's sonnets, for example, well over ninety percent of the lines are composed in masculine rhyme. I have also, occasionally, shortened Pushkin's line, replacing, for example, an Alexandrine or a hexameter with an English pentameter or, more rarely, a pentameter with a tetrameter. The English language, with its many monosyllables, is quite unlike polysyllabic Russian, so retaining all of Pushkin's longer meters seemed unwarranted. Too often it would have called for padding the lines simply in order to fill them out.

I should note that in the Russian many of the poems bear no titles; for the sake of convenient reference I have, therefore, where this is the case, either provided a title or used a first line as such. I have also placed an accent mark in the text on names and certain other words for the reader's convenience, to show where the stress should fall.

Pushkin's work is notoriously elusive for the translator, and on many occasions as I worked on his poems, I had to abandon my efforts, finding many of the lyrics utterly untransferable into English, at least by me. No translation can hope to capture this poet's seamless blend of sound and meaning, or to convey the inimitable musical instrumentation and the precise linguistic properties of his poetry. But the poems given here, which are among those that I have come to admire and love, are also those that I have felt myself in some measure capable of attempting in a tongue rather distant from their own.

I would like to take this opportunity to express my thanks to Henry Carrigan of Northwestern University Press for his support and commitment to this project as well as to Serena Brommel, Marianne Jankowski, and Jenny Gavacs for their care and sensitivity in shepherding this book into print.

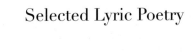

Selected Lyric Poetry

Lyrics

✦ 1813–1819 ✦

Verse written in Pushkin's teenage years,
between the ages of fourteen and nineteen

THE ROSE

Our rose, my friends,
Can it be gone?
A withered bloom,
The child of dawn?
Oh do not cry:
Thus youth must go!
Oh do not sigh:
Life's joy is so!
We'll tell the rose:
Alas, good-bye!
And to the lily
Turn our eye.

Young Daphnis, chasing Chloe, cried:
"My beauty, wait! Don't run away!
Just say: I love you—don't go hide,
I swear by Venus, I won't stay!"
"Be silent!" Reason coldly said;
"Say: I adore you!" Eros pled.

"Adore you!" sang the maiden sweet,
And love set both their hearts ablaze,
And Daphnis fell before her feet,
And Chloe dropped her flaming gaze.
"Oh flee! Oh flee!" cold Reason cried,
While crafty Eros "Stay!" replied.

She stayed. And, trembling with his love,
The happy shepherd made his plea:
"Oh look," he said, "that downy dove
Has kissed his mate beneath the tree!"
"Oh flee!" cried Reason once again;
"They'll show you how!" said Eros then.

At last a tender smile spilled
Across the blushing maiden's lips,
And as her eyes with languor filled
Within her lover's arms she slipped.
"Be happy!" Eros softly said.
And Reason's words? Oh, Reason fled.

MY EPITAPH

Here Pushkin lies at rest; in indolence and love,
And with the tender Muse, he spent his happy span;
He never did much good, but still at heart he was
    A decent sort of man.

And so I happy was and reveled in life's kiss,
Both quiet joys I knew and days of deepest bliss—
    But where did all such pleasures fly?
    Those dreams and visions did not last,
    My heady blisses faded fast,
And round me once again, ennui's grim shadows lie! . . .

All lies veiled in solemn silence;
Darkness wraps the hill in shrouds;
Pale young moon meanders idly
Past a bank of gleaming clouds.
Down below a noble lord
Lies inside his quiet tomb;
Now and then a doleful chord,
Sweet as languid love's reward,
Echoes from that lifeless room.
O'er the grave: a dove and lyre,
Bowls of roses, laurel wreath—
Friends, the sage of sensual fire,
Gone forever, lies beneath.
How the carver's art succeeded:
How that marble seems to breathe!
Hear his plea for one more day,
See him gaze within the glass,
Crying out: "I'm old and gray!
Life is far too fleet, alas!"
Palms upraised to touch the lyre,
On his brow a frown of dread,
He would sing of sword and fire—
Sings of nought but love instead.
Now the sage prepares to pay
Nature's last and greatest debt;
Still he dances, stooped and gray,
Crying out and thirsting yet.
Round about the gray-haired lover
Maidens dance to lilting song;

How from miser time he covets
Brief reprieve, one moment long!
Now the Muses, now the Graces,
Dance their darling to his tomb;
Ivy twines about their faces,
Roses in their tresses bloom.
Now he's gone, like every pleasure—
Gone like love and like its kiss.
Wretched mortals, life's a specter:
Seize the fleeting time of bliss!
Revel, revel, in your fashion,
Fill the glass as oft you can,
Rend your hearts with flames of passion,
Greet the night with cup in hand!

TO NATASHA

Summer's beauty starts to fade,
Sunlit days are fleeing fast;
Late at night in drowsy shade
Chilling mists go floating past.
Empty now the fields of gold,
Playful brooks are still and cold;
Curly woods grow gray and grim,
Heaven's vault itself is dim.

Sweet Natasha, lovely flower!
Why has no one seen your face?
Won't you share a single hour
With your love in soft embrace?
Neither near the water's billows,
Nor beneath the weeping willows,
Neither early, no, nor late
Have I met my pretty mate.

Soon the winter's chill will blight
Field and forest, grove and glen;
Soon the blazing hearth I'll light
Deep inside my smoky den.
Then I'll see my love no more;
Locked away behind my door,
Like a captive bird I'll pine—
Sweet Natasha on my mind.

A WINDOW

Not long ago in dead of night,
When through the mist the moonbeams shone,
Beneath the solemn rays of light
I saw a maiden all alone
Before a window lost in thought;
Her bosom rose in secret dread
As with her nervous eyes she sought
The pathway through the hills ahead.

An urgent whisper came: "I'm here!"
And with a trembling hand the maid
Drew up the window, filled with fear . . .
And then the moon was lost in shade.
"You happy man!" I murmured low,
"A joyful night has come for thee;
But when will moon and darkness show
A window opened thus for me?"

Did you not hear, within the grove by night,
The voice of love, the singer of his woes?
And when at dawn from silent fields arose
A reed-pipe's song in melancholy plight,
    Did you not hear?

Did you not meet, within a darkened lair,
The voice of love, the singer of his grief?
A trace of tears, a smile soft and brief,
A gaze of anguish and of bleak despair,
    Did you not meet?

Did you not sigh, attending to that sound,
The voice of love, the singer of his lay?
And when at last you saw the youth that day
And looked into the lightless eyes you found,
    Did you not sigh?

TO MORPHEUS

Sweet Morpheus, until the morn
Bring joy to love's tormented state;
Extinguish now this lamp forlorn
And grant my dreams a happy fate!
Conceal from mournful memory's ken
The dreaded verdict of *adieu*!
Come, let me see those eyes again,
Come, let me hear the voice I knew.
And when the dark of night has fled
And your command of eyelids ends,
Oh could my soul of love be shed
Until once more the night descends!

TO FRIENDS

The gods will grant you yet, my friends,
Full many golden nights and days,
And languid maidens' eyes will bend
On you their long and searching gaze.
Play on and sing your songs, my friends!
Partake of fleeting evening's bliss;
And through these tears of mine I'll send
Your carefree joys a smile's kiss.

When I to pay my homage
Set sail to ancient Paphos,
I actually encountered
In Aphrodite's chamber
Anacreon's last chalice,
Still filled with wine and foaming.
Around the bowl hung myrtle,
Green ivy vines and roses,
Their branches twined and woven
By Aphrodite's fingers.
And on the lip I noted
A deeply mournful Eros,
Who sat there gazing sadly
At all the foaming liquid.
"Why, cherub, are you staring
At all the foaming liquid?"
I asked the doleful Cupid,
"And tell me, why so quiet?
And why you spurn a ladle
And only dip your fingers?"
"Oh, no," the prankster answered,
"While playing in that ocean
I dropped my bow and arrows,
And in those scarlet billows
My flaming torch has guttered;
They're on the bottom glist'ning,
But I'm, alas, no swimmer.
Oh, what a loss! But listen,
For you can save my quiver!"
"Oh, no," I told the cherub,

"Be grateful that they've fallen
And leave them there forever."

The poem is unrhymed in Russian.

FOR A PORTRAIT OF KAVERIN

In him burn ever hot the flames of punch and war;
Upon the fields of Mars a fearsome man of duty,
A faithful friend to friends, a goad to charming beauty,
    And lancer to the core.

Peter Kaverin (1794–1858), hussar and man of letters, friend of Pushkin.

FOR AN ALBUM

Our love will pass, our passions die;
The frigid world will part us, too.
And who recalls the secret sighs,
The dreams and ecstasies they knew? . . .
So let these leaves of recollection
Preserve their slender trace of you.

SIGN ON A HOSPITAL WALL

Here lies a student gravely ill;
His lot is only to endure.
So take away that useless pill:
There is for love as yet no cure!

Orlóv completely naked lay
Beside Istómina in bed,
But when it came to torrid play,
This sorry general never led.
Not wishing to offend him, she
Took up her microscope and said:
"If you don't mind, I'd like to see
Just what you used in screwing me."

Alexey Orlov (1786–1861), Russian general; Avdotya Istomina (1799–1848), a famous ballerina.

TO OGAREVA, TO WHOM THE BISHOP
SENT SOME FRUIT FROM HIS GARDEN

The Bishop, shameless braggart he,
In sending you his garden's fruits,
Has clearly sought to make us see
That he's the god of his pursuits.

All hail to you—your beauty's grace
Will conquer even wretched age;
You'll drive the Bishop mad apace
And make his fiery passions rage.

Once having seen your magic gaze,
He'll soon forget the cross above
To sing a tender hymn of praise
To your celestial beauty, love.

The references are to Elizaveta Ogareva (1786–1870), society belle, and the
Bishop of St. Petersburg.

TO CHADAYEV

Not long did glory, hope, or love,
Those sweet deceits of life, exist;
The joys of youth were soon undone,
Like visions or the morning mist.
But still within us passions breed;
Beneath oppressive Fate we stand
And with impatient souls we heed
The summons of our native land.
We wait with yearning's expectation
For sacred Freedom's coming light
The way a lover waits at night
To consummate an assignation.
And while we burn with Freedom's thirst,
And while our hearts for honor live,
Unto the land that gave us birth
The raptures of our souls we give.
Believe, my friend, the star will rise,
That captivating joy we crave:
Our Russia will awake with pride,
And on the tyrant's bloody grave
Our names, my friend, will be inscribed.

Peter Chadayev (1798–1856), friend of Pushkin, a philosopher and sharp critic
of Russian backwardness. His belief that Russia's future lay with the values
of western European civilization helped to create the great divide between
Westernizers and Slavophiles in Russian thought.

TO ZHUKOVSKY

When reaching for the world of dreams,
Your lofty spirit all afire,
Impatiently upon your knees
You hold with restless hand the lyre.
When in the magic dark you see
Fleet visions pass before your eyes,
And inspiration's chilling breeze
Makes all your hair in dread arise,
You're right, you sing for just the few
And not for jealous connoisseurs
Or all that wretched, carping crew
Who love to parrot what they've heard,
But only for the loyal friends
Of sacred truth and talent's ends.
Good fortune doesn't shine on all,
Not all were born to wear a wreath;
But blest who hears the subtle call
Of lofty thought and poet's speech!
Who took delight in beauty's spell
When beauty hovered near
And understood the joy you felt
With joy as fierce and clear.

Vassily Zhukovsky (1783–1852), poet and translator of Western poets, leader of the Russian Romantic school. A friend and mentor to Pushkin, with his connections at court (he was tutor to the future Czar Alexander II) he was often able to intercede with the Emperor on the poet's behalf.

FOR A PORTRAIT OF ZHUKOVSKY

The captivating sweetness of his lines
Will long outlive the envy of an age,
And hearing them bright youth will heave a sigh,
Mute sorrow will assuage its bitter pain,
And even giddy joy will ponder life.

TO THE AUTHOR OF *A HISTORY OF THE RUSSIAN STATE*

His *History* gallantly confirms
That autocratic rule is right
And tells us in the simplest terms:
The whip was made for our delight.

Nikolai Karamzin (1766–1826), celebrated historian whose *History of Russia* was a major source for Pushkin's drama *Boris Godunov*. Politically conservative, he nonetheless contributed much to the modernization of the Russian literary language.

HERCULES AND BACCHUS

Hercules and Bacchus
Beg for lusty men;
They and their procuress
Wait for us, my friend.
Kegs of wine, and roses,
Bacchus bids us come!
He's already opened
Bottles three of rum.

. . . .

For all my former sins I'm sentenced now to hell:
I've suffered for eight days with potions in my gut.
Despair consumes my brain—and mercury, my blood.
I suffer; and the quack—assures me all is well.

RESURRECTION

The artist-vandal's lazy brush
Besmears a truthful work of art
And in a senseless, drunken rush
Destroys a painting's living heart.

But with the years those painted lies
Like rotting scales are all unpeeled,
And once again before our eyes
A work of genius stands revealed.

So, too, with age there disappear
My soul's transgressions and untruth,
And then once more there reappear
The purest visions of my youth.

DORIDA

Dorída cheers my heart: I love her golden tresses,
The pale blue eyes she has, the face that she possesses . . .
Abandoning my friends, I left the feast last night
And tasted in her arms the fullness of delight:
Fresh ecstasies replaced each ecstasy that dwindled,
And passions quickly slaked were once again rekindled;
I swooned, but in the dim uncertainty of night
Another's lovely form came flooding to my sight,
And stricken with a sad and secret sense of shame,
I heard my lips call out an unexpected name.

Probably refers to Olga Masson (dates unknown), a well-known St. Petersburg
courtesan.

SOLITUDE

Blest he who in his quiet nook,
Far off from every dunce and mope,
Devotes his day to some good book,
To memory, leisure, work, and hope—
Whom fate has sent companions deep,
Who by his Master's grace, it seems,
Is free from bores who make him sleep
And cads who rouse him when he dreams.

FOR A PORTRAIT OF DELVIG

Here comes our Delvig now, the man who always said
That if, by fate's decree, he held a righteous sword,
He'd let foul Nero go, to take off Titus' head,
For Nero even so would reap his just reward.

Anton Delvig (1798–1831), one of Pushkin's closest friends, a poet and publisher,
in whose journal, *Northern Flowers,* many of Pushkin's lyrics appeared.

MERRY FEAST

I commend the merry meal
Where enjoyment reigns as lord,
There where Freedom, my ideal,
Rules the banquet's festive board,
Where till morn the cry *Drink up!*
Drowns the drunken songs we sing,
Where the guests in concert sup,
Where the jostling bottles ring.

In vain, my tender friend, my heart deceived in love;
I struggled to conceal the coldness deep within.
You understood me, though—enchantment came undone;
    My love for you grew dim.
All rapture and delight departed on that day:
    The time of wonder fled,
    All longings passed away,
    My youthful hopes lay dead.

FRAGMENTS

*

A garland cap of roses,
Uncovered breast and lace,
And over one white shoulder
A shawl was loosely draped.

To Denis Davydov

A fellow eloquent and quarrelsome,
A rake and ardent poet.

*

You ask me to unseal my soul—
I dared to worship from afar,
But passion overwhelmed my heart.

*

Set down, O Lesbia, the lamp
Where love has made her tranquil couch.

Denis Davydov (1784–1839), hussar and poet, hero of the War of 1812.

Lyrics

✦ 1820–1829 ✦

Verse written when the poet was in his twenties

I've known the saber's joyous sound:
A devotee of martial fame,
I love the bloody battleground,
And thoughts of death my soul inflame.
Whoever in his flowery youth,
As freedom's knight, took death amiss,
Has never tasted joy, in truth,
Nor well deserved a maiden's kiss.

GOOD ADVICE

Let's raise our glasses and be merry,
Let's savor life and so be glad;
We'll let the blind and foolish worry—
It's not for us to ape the mad.
Let flighty youth be drowned in bliss,
In foaming wine, and in life's feast;
Let fickle joy bestow its kiss
On all our days, in dreams at least.
When youth, like smoke, has fled the dell
And hastened youthful joys away,
Then we shall take from age as well
Whatever age may cast our way.

ELEGY
(In Imitation of Byron)

Adieu, adieu, my native land!
Lord Byron

The lamp of day grows dim and fails;
The evening mists across the ocean sweep.
Resound, resound! Fill up, responsive sails,
Come, stir yourself beneath me, sullen deep!

I see a distant shore ahead,
The southern lands of some enchanted place,
And with my thirsting spirit, there I race
    While mem'ries charm my giddy head . . .
I feel my eyes well up again with tears;
    My heart now soars, now seems to drown,
As old familiar visions hover round.
I recollect the loves of other years,
Both all I've suffered and the joyful tales,
The dreams and vanished hopes that made me weep . . .
Resound, resound! Fill up, responsive sails,
Come, stir yourself beneath me, sullen deep!

Fly onward, ship, and bear me far away,
Wherever dreadful seas by whim command,
    But not to those sad shores, I pray,
    Of my benighted native land,
    Where flames of passion first were fanned
    And lit emotions in my breast
As by the tender muses I was blest—
    But where my wasted youth was doomed
    To stormy death before it bloomed,

Where light-winged joy betrayed me when it fled
And left my frigid heart unmoved instead.

    A seeker then of new sensation,
    From you I flew, my native clime;
From you I flew, you feeders on temptation,
You fleeting friends of youth's too-fleeting time;
And you, you confidantes of degradation,
To whom, devoid of love, I offered whole
My peace and fame, my freedom and my soul;
From you as well, you faithless ones, I'm moving on,
You secret playmates of my golden dawn.
Farewell to you . . . but in my heart I keep
The wounds of love, for which no cure avails . . .
Resound, resound! Fill up, responsive sails,
Come, stir yourself beneath me, sullen deep.

TO DORIDA

I do believe I'm loved; the heart must live believing.
Oh no, my darling girl could never once deceive me.
No part of her is false: her passion's languid face,
Her manner soft and shy, the precious gift of grace,
Her easiness in speech, the casual way she dresses,
And all the tender words her youthful love professes.

I DO NOT MISS YOU, YOUTHFUL YEARS

I do not miss you, youthful years,
Ill-spent in dreams of love in vain,
Nor you, you dark and secret spheres,
Extolled by passion's mad refrain.

I do not miss you, former friends,
You festive wreaths and foaming glasses,
Nor you, you fond and faithless lasses,
And, pensive, shun amusement's ends.

But where are you, O moments sweet
Of tender hopes and silent tears?
Where now is inspiration's heat?
Oh come again, my youthful years.

NEREID

Amid the jade-green waves that kiss the shores of Tauris
One early morn we saw a Nereid before us.
Concealed among the trees, I held my breath and spied:
Above the sparkling deep, the demigoddess sighed;
Her youthful, swan-white breast bestirred the startled air,
As in a stream she wrung the foam from glist'ning hair.

Nereid, a sea nymph in Greek mythology.

Tauris, an ancient name for the Crimea.

EPIGRAM

Abuse, it seems, can't wear you out!
But let's conclude this sorry tale:
I'm idle, yes, and gad about,
While you work hard to no avail.

The lines are addressed to an unknown critic.

THE BEAUTY IN THE MIRROR

Before her mirror see the charming lass
As she arranges flowers in her hair,
Caressing one stray lock—and how the glass
Reflects her smiling pride and cunning stare.

I've lived to see my longings die:
My dreams and I have grown apart;
Now only sorrows haunt my eye,
The wages of a bitter heart.

Beneath the storms of hostile fate,
My flowery wreath has faded fast;
I live alone and sadly wait
To see when death will come at last.

Just so, when winds in winter moan
And snow descends in frigid flakes,
Upon a naked branch, alone,
The final leaf of summer shakes! . . .

THE MAIDEN

I told you so before: beware the maiden tender!
I knew she had the charm to make all hearts surrender.
O unsuspecting friend! I knew how you'd despise
To notice any other or search another's eyes.
Bereft of every hope, forgetting fleet desire,
Within her clutches youth, grown pensive, turns to fire.
All bléssèd sons of bliss, all favorites of fate,
Quite humbly bear to her their love-besotted state;
But, oh, the haughty maid condemns their foolish tears
And, lowering her eyes, she neither sees nor hears.

TO NIKOLAI ALEKSEEV
(On Sending Him *The Gabrieliad*)

She's here, the Muse, that playful sprite,
The one you used to love so well.
My naughty girl is now contrite
That she succumbed to courtly spells;
Almighty God did lately lay
His regal hand upon her head—
And she has turned from risky play
To righteous enterprise instead.
You mustn't, friend, display surprise
To see her in Israeli guise;
Forgive her youthful sins remote
And, under its new sacred seal,
Accept this poignant verse she wrote.

Nikolai Alekseev (1788–1854), friend of Pushkin.

The Gabrieliad is a ribald excursion on biblical themes.

FOR A PORTRAIT OF CHADAYEV

By one of heaven's high decrees
He entered life to serve the Czar;
In Rome—he'd Brutus be, in Athens—Pericles,
    But here—a mere hussar.

See earlier note on Chadayev.

MY VOICE WILL SOON GROW MUTE

My voice will soon grow mute. But if on that sad day
The pensive strings might call and answer me in play;
If only youthful friends, attending to my rhymes,
Might wonder how I stood love's anguish and commotion;
If only you yourself, succumbing to emotion,
Would whisper in the dark my melancholy lines
And honor with your love the discourse of my heart;
If only I were loved—I'd ask you as we part
To let me bring to life my singing at the end
With your most sacred name, my beauty and my friend.
And after I have gone to my eternal rest,
Then say above my grave, with feeling in your breast:
I loved him at the last and gave him all my heart,
For I was then his muse of passion and of art.

ONE FINAL TIME

One final time, my tender friend,
I steal into your room like this;
One final time with you I'll spend
In raptures of untroubled bliss.

Henceforth, amid the dark of night,
Await me not in languid shame;
Before the dawn, no longer light
   A candle flame.

EPIGRAM ON A. A. DAVYDOVA

Agláya gave herself to one
Because she liked his scarlet sash,
And to a Frenchman just for fun,
And someone else for simple cash,
To Cleon for his noble brow,
And Damis for the verse he read.
But tell me, dear Agláya, how
Your husband got you into bed?

Aglaya Davydova (1787–1842) was the promiscuous wife of General A. L.
Davydov. Pushkin had a brief affair with her, but the lady's condescending
manner irritated his sense of pride. Subsequently he made her the subject of
several spiteful epigrams.

ON KACHENOVSKY

A slanderer with empty head,
He blindly gropes for any brick
And tries to earn his daily bread
With monthly lies that never stick.

Mikhail Kachenovsky (1775–1842), editor of a monthly journal, *The Herald of Europe,* and a journalistic foe of Pushkin's.

TO MY FRIENDS

Last night we held a farewell revel,
A bacchanalian feast of fire;
Insane with youth, we hailed the devil,
We toasted life and played the lyre.

And how the muses blessed you, brothers,
And sent you garlands from above,
When you, dear friends, before all others,
Bestowed on me your cup of love.

The cup itself did not astound me
With all the noble gilt it wore,
Nor did its workmanship confound me,
Those crystal carvings that it bore.

One thing alone drew my attention:
That, fashioned for a thirsty beast,
That cup, gigantic in dimension,
Could hold a bottle's worth at least.

I drank—and on a flood of feeling
I floated back to former days,
And I recalled, my senses reeling,
The grief of life when love decays.

And my delusions set me laughing,
And sorrow vanished from my side,
The way the froth in foaming glasses
Will vanish in the rushing tide.

PRISONER

I sit in my cell where the windows are barred.
An eagle is feeding below in the yard;
A sullen companion, a captive like me,
He tears at the blood-covered carcass I see.

He tears and he scatters it; eyeing my cell,
He seems to be thinking of freedom as well.
His look catches mine and his cry seems to say:
"Let's both take a chance and let's both fly away!

We're birds of the air and it's time that we fly
Far off where the cloud-covered mountaintops lie,
Far over the sea where the breezes and I
Will roam as we will the cerulean sky!"

While serving in southern Russia, Pushkin spent a short time in jail because of a duel. Duels, although proscribed, were common at the time, and Pushkin, who was notoriously touchy about his honor, was quick to offer a challenge.

TO A FOREIGN LADY

In language you won't comprehend
I write this verse to say good-bye;
And yet it's pleasant to pretend
That you might read my cryptic lines.
Until, my friend, the day I die,
Undone at last by parting's rue,
I'll never cease to long and sigh
For you, my friend, and only you.
And when on foreign eyes you gaze,
Believe no heart but mine, my dear,
As once before you placed your faith
In one whose love you couldn't hear.

"You're off? The country, I suppose,
To breathe the bracing morning air
And with your dreamy muse to doze
In solitude, without a care?"
"Why, no—I'm headed for the fair;
I like the bustle of bazaars,
The varied crowd encountered there:
The skull-capped Jew, the bearded Slav,
Their shouts and cries, the hawkers' stalls,
The free and greedy, raucous mob."
"So you observe and thus assess
In such a place the people's mood;
I'd quite enjoy it, I confess,
To go along and hear your views,
But duty calls and I must pass—
We haven't time for fun, alas."
"So where will you—?"
"The dungeon, friend; today, you see,
We're sending under lock and key
Across Moldavia's frontier
. . . the outlaw Kirdzhalí."

George Kirdzhali, a Greek patriot and rebel against the Turks.

A SMALL BIRD

In foreign lands I like to keep
A custom from my land of birth:
I set a captive warbler free
To mark when spring returns to earth.

And then I feel within this breast
My somber heart and spirits lift.
Why rant at God when you are blest
To give one creature such a gift!

WHO WAS IT, WAVES?

Who was it, waves, that made you cease?
Who chained your mighty waters' stride?
Who made of your great rushing tide
A placid pond of drowsy peace?
Whose magic wand in passing stole
My sorrows, joys, and hot desires?
Who lulled to sleep my stormy soul
And banked my ardent youthful fires?
Come roar, you winds, come lash the deep!
Destroy this fatal castle keep!
Where are you, storm—you foe of slaves?
Come rouse and stir these captive waves!

NIGHT

My voice for thee, my love, with languorous caresses
Disturbs the solemn peace the midnight dark possesses.
Beside this couch of mine a mournful candle glows,
And, welling up, my verse in rippling murmurs flows;
It flows in streams of love, its music wholly thine,
And in the dark thine eyes are sparkling over mine.
They look at me and smile—and, oh, the sounds I hear:
"My sweet and tender friend . . . my love . . . my dear,
    my dear."

This is one of several poems dedicated to Amalia Riznich (1803–25), a married woman with whom Pushkin had a passionate love affair in Odessa during his exile in the south of Russia. She gave birth to a child that Pushkin thought he might have fathered, and shortly thereafter, because of poor health, she left Russia for Italy, where she died a year later in her early twenties. Apparently, the child soon died as well.

THE DEMON

In former days when I was thrilled
By each new vision life supplied:
A maiden's glance, a wooded hill,
The song of nightingales at night—
When all my lofty aspirations
For freedom, fame, and faithful love,
And art with all its inspirations
So roused my soul and stirred my blood—
Those days of hope and sweet delight
Were overwhelmed by sudden anguish
When secretly an evil genius
Began to visit me at night.
Our meetings were morose and bleak:
His grin, the probing looks he stole,
The bitter words I heard him speak
Instilled a venom in my soul.
With inexhaustible invective
He tempted Fate with open eyes;
He labeled beauty but a specter,
And inspiration he despised.
Distrusting love and its salvation,
He looked at life with mocking gaze
And so denied to all creation
His blessing or a word of praise.

This poem seems to have been inspired by Alexander Raevsky (1795–1868), a military man who became friendly with Pushkin during the poet's exile in the south. He was apparently a baneful influence on the young Pushkin as well as his rival for the affections of Countess Vorontsova, whom they both courted.

Behold, a sower went forth to sow.

Before the morning star I passed
Across the land with freedom's seed;
From chaste and guiltless hand I cast
Into the furrows long in need
The life-bestowing germ I brought—
But time and labor went for nought,
A well-intended, futile deed . . .

Graze on, submissive peoples—sleep!
You will not wake to honor's call.
What use are freedom's gifts to sheep?
Their lot—the shears and slaughter stall;
Their legacy lies rooted deep:
The whistling lash, the chain and ball.

The epigraph comes from Matthew 13:3.

IT'S OVER

It's over, we are finished, you and I.
Embracing for that final time your knees,
I uttered only melancholy pleas.
It's over—I can hear your voice reply.
I won't deceive again my foolish heart,
Nor will I now inflict my pain on you:
Perhaps I can forget the joy I knew—
And recognize that love and I must part.
But you are young—and beautiful in spirit,
And you shall yet be loved by many men.

This is another poem dedicated to Amalia Riznich. The last two lines of the poem do not rhyme in Russian.

TO CHADAYEV
(From the Crimean Seacoast)

What use is cold and doubting thought?
A dreadful temple crowned this site
Where once the greedy gods were brought
The blood of human sacrifice;
For thus did savage man appease
The fierce and dread Eumenides,
And here their priestess on command
Against her brother raised her hand.
But where these ancient ruins lie
The sacred cause of friendship won,
And two great souls awoke with pride
·To see the savage gods undone.

. . . .

Chadáyev, can you see those days
When long ago in happy youth
We censured with a fateful name
Another ruin's bloodied truth?
But in my heart, subdued by strife,
More feebly burn those former flames;
Yet moved by this great gift of life,
Upon this stone where friendship blazed,
I stoop, my friend, to write our names.

Pushkin, while traveling in the Crimea, had visited the supposed site of an
ancient temple of Artemis, and the occasion resulted in this poem. The temple
was connected to the myth of Orestes, the son of Agamemnon: Pursued by
the Eumenides (the Furies) for the sin of slaying his mother, Clytemnestra
(to avenge her murder of his father), Orestes makes his way to the Crimea,

where both he and his loyal friend, Pylades, are taken captive and condemned to be sacrificed to the goddess. The high priestess of the temple, who is forced to perform the sacrifice, turns out to be Iphigenia, Orestes' long-lost sister, although at first the two do not recognize each other. When they do eventually learn each other's identities, Orestes and his sister, along with Pylades, make their escape and sail away.

ON COUNT VORONTSOV

Half English lord, half merchant-cheat,
Half pompous sage, half silly dope,
Half scoundrel, too, but here there's hope
That he'll at last become complete.

Count Mikhail Vorontsov (1782–1856), governor of southern Russia and
Pushkin's superior in the state service. Pushkin's hostile relations with the
Anglophile count were further complicated by his love affair with the count's
wife, Elizaveta Vorontsova (1792–1880).

TEMPEST

You saw a maiden on a cliff
Above the sea, all dressed in white
As, raging in the stormy mist,
The waves and shore were locked in fight;
As bolts of lightning flashed and poured
A crimson glow about her shape;
As round her head the tempest roared
And winds assailed her streaming cape.
O splendid sea and storm and mist!
O gleaming heavens flashing free!
And yet that maiden on the cliff
Outshines that sky and storm and sea.

AQUILON

I wonder why, dread Aquilon,
You drive the reeds against the land?
And why in fury you pursue
That cloudlet through the heavens' span?

Not long ago the vaulting sky
In black and angry clouds was chained;
Not long ago above the heights
The oak in haughty beauty reigned.

But you arose and, seething, roared,
And in your raging glory spoke—
You scattered all the tempest's hordes
And brought to earth the mighty oak.

Now let the sun display his face
To shine with joy in all the skies.
Let zephyr with that cloudlet play
And let the gentle reeds arise.

Aquilon, god of the North Wind, here a reference to the Emperor.

TO ALEXEY VULF

Greetings, Vulf, my trusty friend!
Come while winter snows descend.
In your sleigh along with you
Drag the bard Yazýkov, too.
Over fields we'll ride on horse,
Try our pistols out, of course.
Curly-headed Lionél
(Not that local clerk of mine)—
He'll provide for us quite well . . .
What? A case of bottled wine!
Hush! We'll feast us while we may,
Live like happy anchorites,
At Trigórskoye all day,
At Mikháilovskoye nights.
We'll by day in love be sunk,
Then at night our glasses raise;
We'll be either deadly drunk
Or in love's besotted daze.

These lines were part of a letter that Pushkin sent to his friend, Alexey Vulf
(1805–81), whose family's estate of Trigorskoye was near the Pushkin estate of
Mikhailovskoye. Vulf at the time was a student at Dorpat University, as was the
poet Nikolai Yazykov (1803–46), another of Pushkin's friends. "Lionel" refers to
Pushkin's younger brother, Lev (Leo).

The stormy day is spent, and now the murk of night
Extends across the sky its leaden-colored cape;
Behind the grove of firs now looms a spectral shape—
    The moon in pallid light.
A deep and somber ache has settled on my soul
While far away the moon completes its bright ascent,
While far away the air grows warm in evening's tent,
While far away the seas in splendid billows roll
    Beneath an azure sky . . .
And now the time has come: she's walking down the hill
To wander by the shore, where rushing waters spill,
    Where cherished boulders lie . . .
She's sitting now, all sad, alone beside the sea—
Alone . . . with none to weep, or languish in her eyes;
With none to kiss her knees in adoration tender;
Alone—to no one's kiss does she tonight surrender
Her shoulders, dewy lips, and breasts of snowy splendor.
Oh, none deserves the bliss that she, in love, can give.
Oh, say it's so: that you're alone—and I can live.
but if . . .

Another poem addressed to Amalia Riznich.

Let one now crowned with love and beauty's cherished bliss
Preserve in hallowed gold the features he would kiss
And all the private notes that sweeten separation.
But in these silent days of parting's desolation
There's nothing on this earth to cheer my haunted gaze:
No single gift she made in once enraptured days,
No sacred pledge of love, no tender, sad refrain
Can heal this wounded love that's hopeless and insane.

TO A CHILD

My child, I would never dare
To offer you my benedictions.
Your very glance and peaceful air
Are seraphim to my afflictions.

May all your days be ever bright,
As bright as is your glance today.
Amid the happy lots in life
May yours be full of joy, I pray.

Some Russian scholars believe that the child referred to is the one which Pushkin believed to be his own, by Amalia Riznich.

GRAPES

I do not rue the roses late
That faded with the breath of spring;
I also love the viny grape
Whose clusters to the hillside cling,
Those glories of my fertile vale,
The golden autumn's joy displayed,
As slender and translucent-pale
As fingers of a tender maid.

Awake, timid hermit:
Inside of your cave
The lamp of the Prophet
Till morning will blaze.
Abandon your sorrow
And banish your fear;
Give thanks for tomorrow
And be of good cheer!
Till morning in homage
Repeat holy pleas
And read till the morning
The Book on your knees!

LIZA

Liza is afraid to love;
Maybe, though, it isn't true.
Watch yourselves—our little dove
Could be hiding from our view
Tender passions after all;
Maybe with her bashful gaze
She is seeking to appraise
Which of us might help her fall.

Brought up to sound of marching band,
Our Czar was born to take command.
At Austerlitz our hero fled,
In eighteen-twelve was seized with dread;
Yet still he stayed the war's professor!
But soon he found the front a bore—
And now he works as clerk-assessor
Inside the foreign service corps!

Alexander I, the Czar during the Napoleonic Wars, played a devious political
game: at first he joined the coalition against Napoleonic France; but then, after
Napoleon's victory against the Russians and the Austrians at Austerlitz in 1805,
he became France's ally. War with France resumed after Napoleon invaded
Russia in 1812.

BURNED LETTER

Farewell, love's letter, now! My lady has insisted.
How long I've put it off, how long my hand resisted
Committing all my joy forever to the fire.
But now the time has come: love's letter must expire.
I'm ready now: my heart in resignation grieves,
So let the greedy flames consume your tender leaves.
Ignited! They're ablaze! That puff of smoke I see
Takes with it as it goes my sacred, heartfelt plea;
The waxen seal has lost the faithful finger's mark,
And now it melts and drips, and now, dear God, goes dark!
It's over now—pale leaves in somber ashes rest;
The cherished lines are gone where love was once confessed.
My heart in sorrow breaks. O tender ashen heap,
Poor comfort to a soul condemned by fate to weep,
Remain forever here, against this mournful breast . . .

The poem refers to the poet's affair with Countess Elizaveta Vorontsova, wife of Count Vorontsov, governor of southern Russia and Pushkin's supervisor during part of his southern exile.

MADRIGAL

Your demeanor seems a crime,
Out of step with bliss and grace:
Lovely when it's not the time,
Clever where it's not the place.

FRIENDSHIP

What's friendship, then? Inebriation,
A liberal license to offend,
A common indolence and vainness,
Or shameful patronage, my friend?

ANDRÉ CHÉNIER
(Introduction)

Dedicated to N. N. Raevsky

Ainsi, triste et captif, ma lyre
toutefois s'éveillait . . .
A. Chénier

While yet the world's astounded eye
On Byron's urn directs its gaze,
And while his shade by Dante's side
Hears Europe's choral hymns of praise,

I heed another spirit's spell,
A shade bereft of songs and tears,
Who from a bloody scaffold fell
Beneath the earth before his years:

A bard of love, of groves, and peace,
Whose grave with flowers I commend.
As yet unknown, my lyre speaks
And he and you my song attend.

. . . .

These are the opening stanzas of a long poem devoted to André Chénier (1762–94), the French poet who was one of Pushkin's early enthusiasms and who perished on the guillotine during the Terror of the French Revolution. The dedication is to Nikolai Raevsky (1801–43), brother of Alexander Raevsky (see "The Demon") and a good friend of Pushkin's during his southern exile.

USELESS VICES

Loquaciousness I count among the useless vices
And multitudes of words I long ago forswore;
Believe me, friends, it's true: to make the spirit soar,
All words are far too few, where one alone suffices.

PRESERVE MY SOUL

Preserve my soul, my secret charm:
Preserve me in the days of strife,
In desperate days, and days of harm—
You saved me once from sorrow's knife.

When seas in raging anger hurl
Their waves against my helpless arm,
When thunderclouds about me swirl,
Preserve my soul, my secret charm.

When far from home alone I stray,
When battle sounds its fierce alarm,
When peace asserts its stifling sway,
Preserve my soul, my secret charm.

My sacred, sweet, seductive charm,
The magic beacon of my days—
Now darkened, changed, immune to praise—
Preserve my soul, my secret charm.

May recollection's swollen streams
Convey this wounded heart no harm;
Farewell, all longings; sleep, sweet dreams—
Preserve my soul, my secret charm.

O ROSE AND MAIDEN

O rose and maiden, I'm in chains,
Yet suffer in their grip no wrong:
Just so in laurel lair the lark,
That feathered king of sylvan song,
Will serve sweet bondage to remain
Within the lustrous rose's light
To sing to her his soft refrain
Amid the dark and dulcet night.

FOR THE ALBUM OF ZIZI VULF

Friend, should life in time deceive you,
Do not sorrow, do not fret!
Humbly bear the days that grieve you;
Days of joy await you yet.

By the future live our hearts;
Though the present may be drear—
All is fleeting, all departs;
What has passed will then be dear.

Evpraksia ("Zizi") Vulf (1809–83), a young girl who lived near the Pushkin family estate of Mikhailovskoye and with whom the poet flirted when he was there under house arrest from 1824 to 1826. Pushkin became her lover briefly in 1829. In 1836, writing to a friend from Mikhailovskoye on his last visit there, he described her as "a formerly half-ethereal maiden, now a well-fed wife, big with child for the fifth time."

TO RODZYANKO

You promised once that you'd portray
The arch romantic's feet of clay
And crush that atheistic cur,
Along with all his bag of tricks;
But all you do is write of *Her*—
Ah, no, it's all too clear, good sir,
You've fallen like a ton of bricks!

You're right, of course: what greater prize
Exists on earth than Woman's Beauty?
Her curving lips and gleaming eyes
Compel us more than moral duty,
Than even gold or praise of men—
And so let's talk of *Her* again.

I praise her ready inclination,
With hardly any rest, to bear
A crop of children like their mother;
And happy he who gets to share
Her most delightful occupation,
So much less dull than any other.
And yet—his pleasure may be brief
If Hymen wakes to bring him grief.

But still, I think I disagree
With your approval of divorce,
Since first of all, the laws decree—
And God and nature, too, of course . . .
And secondly, you might recall
That clever ladies do depend
On proper husbands held in thrall,

The sort for whom the "family friend"
Goes hardly noticed, if at all.
I tell you, brothers, it's no lie,
Our fates are plotted high above:
The Sun of marriage blinds the eye
To cloak the bashful Star of love.

Arkady Rodzyanko (1793–1846), Ukrainian poet and friend of Pushkin.

TO ANNA KERN

I still recall a wondrous vision:
That day when I beheld your face,
A fleeting moment's apparition
Of perfect beauty and of grace.

Whenever hopeless grief oppressed me
Amid life's cares and pointless schemes,
Your gentle voice and soul caressed me,
Your cherished features filled my dreams.

The years went by. Fate's storms and stresses
Dispersed those sacred dreams of grace,
And I forgot those soft caresses,
Your gentle voice and angel's face.

In bleak despair and isolation
My days stretched on in quiet strife:
No awe of God, no inspiration,
No love, no tears, no sense of life.

And now once more I've seen that vision:
My soul awoke; I saw your face,
A fleeting moment's apparition
Of perfect beauty and of grace.

My spirit soars in exaltation,
And once again there reappears
The awe of God . . . and inspiration . . .
The sense of life . . . and love . . . and tears.

Anna Kern (1800–1879), whom Pushkin met while living at his country estate of
Mikhailovskoye and with whom he reportedly had an affair.

SAPPHO

O happy, happy youth, you dazzle me with charm:
With ardent, gentle heart, with noble manly pride,
With beauty that recalls a fresh and blushing bride.

Sappho, famous seventh-century B.C. woman poet from the Greek island of Lesbos.

MOVEMENT

No thing can move, the sage averred.
His neighbor simply stood and moved.
A clever answer, all concurred—
And thought the matter subtly proved.
But, sirs, this entertaining tale
Reminds me of another case:
Each day we see the sun set sail,
But Galileo's still in place.

NIGHTINGALE AND CUCKOO

In woods, at night, spring's lover sobs,
He warbles, burbles, trills, and throbs;
He has a dozen songs or more.
The cuckoo, though, that silly bird,
That quite conceited, babbling bore,
Can only cuckoo one dumb word;
It echoes with its double croak
And cuckoos all our brains askew!
So save us, God, and finally choke
That elegiac cry: coo-coo!

THE BLOOMS OF FALL

The blooms of fall are yet more dear
Than those that blushing May can give.
For when the final buds appear
Sad dreams awake our urge to live;
Thus parting often seems more sweet
Than does the day on which we meet.

MY BLOOD'S INFLAMED

My blood's inflamed with hot desire;
You've seared my heart with passion's fire.
Come kiss me now: your lips on mine
Are sweeter far than myrrh or wine.
So bring your tender face more close
And let me lie in sweet repose,
Until the glowing day will start
And shadows of the night depart.

An imitation of the Song of Solomon.

RECALLING YOU

Recalling you consumes my world:
The music of my lyre's art,
The sobbing of a lovelorn girl,
The tremors of my jealous heart,
The lonely dark and glory's gleam,
The beauty of all shining thought,
And vengeance—that impassioned dream
That bitter suffering has wrought.

WINTER EVENING

Storm o'er heaven darkness pours,
Driving snow in gusting gales;
Now like raging beast it roars,
Now like frightened baby wails;
Now our ancient roof it rocks,
Rustling thatch across the grain,
Now like traveler late it knocks
At our battened windowpane.

Our decrepit hut must seem
Dark and dismal in the night;
Tell me, nanny, what you dream
There beside the fading light.
Does the wailing storm, old friend,
Wear you out with all its noise?
Does your buzzing spindle send
Fitful slumber's fleeting joys?

Come, dear friend of youth, drink up,
Let's recall a better day,
Drown our grief—so where's the cup?
Wine will make our hearts more gay.
Sing me how the bluebird flew
Far beyond the ocean swell;
Sing me how the maiden drew
Water early at the well.

Storm o'er heaven darkness pours,
Driving snow in gusting gales;
Now like raging beast it roars,
Now like frightened baby wails.

Come, dear friend of youth, drink up,
Let's recall a better day—
Drown our grief—so where's the cup?
Wine will make our hearts more gay.

The "friend of youth" is Arina Rodionovna Yakovleva (1758–1828), Pushkin's childhood nanny, who introduced him to the language and legends of Russian fairy tales.

TO FRIENDS

For now, my foes, I will not speak—
And you may think my anger dead,
But I will keep you well in reach
To strike one day at someone's head:
He won't escape my ripping claws
When suddenly I deal the blow.
Just so on high the greedy hawk
Keeps eye on hens and geese below.

EX UNGUE LEONEM

Not long ago I penned in verse a "note"
And sent it into print without my name;
Some critic-clown, responding to it, wrote
A diatribe—anonymous, for shame!
No matter, though, for neither I nor he
Succeeded in our underhanded play:
He knew me by my lion's claws, you see,
While his great ass's ears gave him away.

Ex ungue leonem (Latin): we know the lion by his claws.

WHEN FADING ROSES DIE

When fading roses die,
Their breath ambrosia yields
And airy spirits fly
To far Elysian fields.

And there, where sleepy waves
Forgetfulness convey,
Their aromatic shades
By Lethe's river play.

MELANCHOLY MOON

The melancholy moon in heaven's height
Looks round to meet the morning's rosy hue;
The one is cold, the other, blazing bright;
The bridelike dawn is sparkling in the dew.
The moon went pale before her and it died—
As I, Elvina, did—on meeting you.

Beneath her azure native sky
   She languished and grew ill . . .
And waned at last. Her shade flew by
   And cast a moment's chill;
But twixt us is a great divide
   That I would cross in vain:
From callous lips I learned she died,
   And callous I remain.
And it was she whom I adored,
   Consumed by passion's fires,
With such a wretched, tender horde
   Of mad, intense desires!
Where now is love and where the ache
   In memory of those years?
My soul can find for her poor sake
   No anguish now—no tears.

TO VYAZEMSKY

So, it's the sea, that ancient scourge,
That kindles your poetic fire?
You sing dread Neptune's mighty surge
And praise his trident with your lyre.

But hold your praise: On sea and land,
In this foul age, destruction reigns;
And all the elements show man
A tyrant, traitor, or in chains.

Peter Vyazemsky (1792–1876), Pushkin's friend and a fellow poet.

"The world is mine," said mighty Gold.
"Ah, no, it's mine," the Sword proclaimed.
"I'll buy it all," said mighty Gold.
"I'll take it all," the Sword proclaimed.

THE PROPHET

My spirit, thirsting, wandered lost
The grim and barren desert sand,
And where two ancient pathways crossed
I saw a six-winged seraph stand.
With touch as light as sleep or sighs
His fingers brushed my burning eyes,
And they beheld strange visions blaze
As if with startled eagle's gaze.
He gently touched my stricken ears—
And roused the sounds of distant spheres:
I heard the trembling heavens weep,
The monsters moving through the deep,
The flights of angels in the skies,
The sap in valley vineyards rise.
Then bending to my mouth he ripped
The sinful tongue from out my lips
And all its vain and cunning talk;
And on the mute and lifeless stalk,
His right hand steeped in blood, he flung
A serpent's wise and double tongue.
With sword he clove my breast in two,
And thence my beating heart withdrew,
And thrust inside the gaping hole
A flaming shard of living coal.
I lay like death upon the sand
And heard the Voice of God command:
"Arise, O prophet! Heed My Will;
Proclaim what thou hast seen and heard.

On sea and land thy task fulfill:
To burn men's hearts with Heaven's Word."

Based on Isaiah 6:2–9. At the bottom of this poem Pushkin added the date 8 September (1826), the day on which he met with Nicholas I on his release from exile.

TO MY NANNY

My friend in days devoid of good,
My aging and decrepit dove!
Abandoned in a far-off wood,
You still await me with your love.
Beside the window in the hall,
As if on watch, you sit and mourn;
At times your knitting needles stall
In hands now wrinkled and forlorn.
Through long-deserted gates you peer
Upon the dark and distant way;
Forebodings, anguish, cares, and fear
Constrict your weary breast today.
And you imagine. . . . . . .

STANZAS TO CZAR NICHOLAS I

In hope of glory's kind regard
I look ahead with fearless gaze:
Rebellions and beheadings marred
The dawn of Peter's famous days.

But he with truth attracted hearts,
With learning gentled churlish ways;
He honored Dolgorúki's arts
Above the swordsman's savage frays.

With potent autocratic hand
He boldly sowed the seeds of light,
Did not despise his native land,
And knew full well its destined might.

The scholar's and the hero's role,
The shipwright's, seaman's—were his own,
For with his all-embracing soul
He was the workman on the throne.

So in your lineage take pride
And like your forebear nobly stand;
His firmness be your steady guide,
And shun, like him, a vengeful hand.

This poem, addressed to the new Czar who released him from exile, is full of
hope and optimism. In the belief that he will enjoy the trust and confidence
of the Emperor, Pushkin calls on him to show mercy to the revolutionaries
who in December of 1825 had rebelled against the autocracy. The reference to
Peter the Great as an exemplar of clemency seems odd, but Pushkin no doubt
hoped that Nicholas, like Peter before him, would prove to be a reformer and
modernizer. Dolgoruki was a courtier of Peter the Great, whom the Czar allowed
to speak his mind.

TO THE EMPEROR NICHOLAS I

No sooner was he crowned,
Than he displayed his skill:
He shipped a hundred men to prison tightly bound,
And picked five more to kill.

These bitter lines indicate the Emperor's actual response to the Decembrist
uprising.

TO I. I. PUSHCHIN

My dearest friend from long ago!
I too have blessed and thanked my fate
When my secluded portico,
Half buried in the mournful snow,
Announced your sleigh bell at the gate.

Now holy Providence, I plead:
Allow my distant voice to send
Your soul a like relief in need,
And to your prison may it speed
Our glowing lycée days, my friend.

Ivan Pushchin (1798–1859) was one of Pushkin's closest friends and a fellow
student at the imperial lycée. Pushkin recalls here the occasion when Pushchin
visited him during his exile in Mikhailovskoye. The poet sent him this verse after
he was imprisoned for his participation in the Decembrist revolt.

A REPLY

She's no Circassian maid, my friend,
But Georgia's dales have never seen
A beauty such as this descend
From gloomy peak to meadow green.

No agate shines within her gaze,
Yet all the pearls of eastern lands
Could not eclipse the limpid rays
Her lambent southern eyes command.

O spring, O time of love's unrest,
How grave I find your apparition,
What languid stirrings of ambition
Infect my blood and fill my breast!
How foreign to my heart is gladness,
And all that sparkles and exults
Brings only spleen and languid sadness . . .

. . . .

Oh give me blizzards and the snow,
The long, cold dark of winter nights.

THE NIGHTINGALE AND THE ROSE

The nightingale in spring, amid the dark of night,
Erupts in silver song as near the rose he weeps.
But, oh, the tender rose ignores the singer's plight;
Beneath the hymn of love she drifts away and sleeps.

Don't you as well entreat cold beauty with your song?
O poet, have more sense, why vainly weep and long?
Her heart remains unmoved and feels no bliss at all;
She blossoms when you look, but never heeds your call.

TO EK. USHAKOVA

Far away from you, my prize,
I will not forget,
Languid lips and languid eyes—
They'll torment me yet;
Pining in my quiet cell,
I'll reject all cheer.
Will you sigh for me as well
If they hang me, dear?

Ekaterina Ushakova (1809–72), a young beauty whom Pushkin courted in the
late 1820s; he may have contemplated proposing marriage to her.

THREE SPRINGS

In all this world's grim, vasty wastes
Three springs with secret force abound:
The spring of youth that seethes and hastes,
That bubbles, sparkles—full of sound;
Castalia's font, whose waters bring
To banished souls a sweet repast;
And chill oblivion's final spring,
That slakes the fevered heart at last.

ARION

A crowd we were that filled the boat:
Some hoisted sails in arching sweep,
While others with a rhythmic stroke
Set mighty oars against the deep.
Our skillful helmsman at the wheel
In silence steered the laden keel,
While I—with ready trust, at ease—
Sang to the crew. But then the breeze
Turned roaring gale—and roused the seas!
The helmsman and the crew were lost,
While I, strange singer, I was tossed
By raging waves upon the shore,
And here beneath the sun I stand
To dry my cloak upon the sand
And sing the songs I sang before.

The poem seems to refer, obliquely, to the ill-fated Decembrist uprising of 1825, with which Pushkin sympathized and whose participants included several of his friends and acquaintances. After the failure of the coup many of the rebels were executed or imprisoned, whereas Pushkin, who was in exile at the time and away from the capital where the revolt took place, escaped possible punishment. In the poem he likens himself to Arion, the dithyrambic poet of ancient Greece who, according to legend, was miraculously saved from drowning by a dolphin that bore him on his back to shore.

ANGEL

At Eden's gates, with lowered head,
A gentle Angel shed her light,
As up from Hell's abyss there sped
A rebel Demon black as night.

The Shade of doubt and of negation
Upon that sacred spirit gazed
And trembled with a new sensation,
As in him warmth unbidden blazed.

"Farewell!" he cried, "I've seen thine eyes,
Whose light has filled me not in vain:
Not all in Heaven I despise,
Not all on Earth do I disdain."

TO THE PORTRAITIST KIPRENSKY

The mold of form and fashion's cue,
Though not from French or English parts,
Magician, you have made anew
This humble servant of the arts—
And having fled these mortal chains,
I mock the grave and all its claims.

As in a glass I see my face,
A glass that renders me more fair:
It claims that I shall not debase
The passions that the Muses share.
And thus henceforth shall I be known
To Dresden, Paris, and to Rome.

Orest Kiprensky (1782–1836), the artist who in 1827 painted a portrait of Push-
kin commissioned by the poet's friend, Anton Delvig.

THE POET

Until Apollo calls the bard
To holy sacrifice again,
He lives immersed, without regard,
In all the petty cares of men.
His hallowed harp is rendered dumb,
His sleeping spirit lies unblest,
And mid this world's unworthy sons,
He may be worse than all the rest.

But once his heedful ear partakes
Of that divine inspiring word,
The poet's dormant soul is stirred
And like a mighty eagle wakes.
Grown weary of the world's dull ways,
Abandoning the babbling crowd,
He spurns the idols people praise
And holds his haughty head unbowed.
Gone fierce and savage, off he flees,
Consumed with madness and with sound,
To shores where vacant waves abound,
To woodlands and their rustling trees.

Most bléssèd to the golden few
The poet whom the Czar attends.
Both tears and laughter are his due,
As lies with bitter truth he mends.
His verses tickle jaded tastes
When boyar pride his humor wastes;
Embellishing their festive days
He only hears their clever praise.
But just outside the heavy gates
In huddled masses, checked and barred,
The people, grumbling at the fates,
Attend the poet from afar . . .

The boyars were members of an older Russian noble class; here Pushkin
presumably has in mind the state authorities and other sycophants around the
throne.

19 OCTOBER 1827

God grant you, friends, a helping hand—
In cares of state and private plights,
In rowdy feasts of friendship's band,
In passion's sweet and secret rites!

God grant you, friends, a helping hand—
In daily woes and days of strife,
On vacant sea, in distant land,
In every black abyss of life!

The 19th of October was the date (in 1811) on which the Emperor Alexander I established the lycée at one of his palaces; its purpose was to train sons of the nobility for state service. Pushkin studied there from 1811 to 1817, and he often marked the anniversary of this date with a poem for a celebration with fellow former students. The town where the school was located was known then as Tsarskoye Selo (The Czar's Village); it is named today after Pushkin.

I KNOW A LAND

I know a land where on the shore
The seas in lonely splendor run,
Where snows are almost never found,
Where from a cloudless sky the sun
Ignites the burning meadow ground;
There are no trees—above the sea
Alone the naked steppes abound.

TO DAWE, ESQ.

Why use your wonder-working pen
To draw this Moorish face of mine?
Though it be meant for future men,
It's sure to make the devil whine.

So draw Olénina, I pray:
When inspiration fans the heart,
Then youth and beauty, only they,
Should summon genius to its art.

George Dawe (1781–1829), British portrait painter at the Russian court.

Anna Olenina (1808–88), a young lady whom Pushkin courted in the late 1820s.

REMEMBRANCE

When day for mortal men in silence ends,
And over all the city's quiet squares
The half-transparent shade of night descends,
And sleep knits up the day with all its cares,
Within the hush to me the hours bring
An agonizing sleeplessness instead:
Amid the idle night the serpent's sting
Torments me with a looming sense of dread;
Dark visions seethe and floods of anguished thought
Assault the very corners of my soul;
Remembrance, then, in silent shadows wrought,
Unravels to my eyes her lengthy scroll;
And reading with disgust the sum of years
I tremble as I curse the fatal signs
And murmur bitter plaints with bitter tears,
But will not wash away those grievous lines.

I see how I have spent in idle days,
In frenzied feasts, in mad unbridled strife,
In poverty of soul, in slavish ways,
And in a wilderness, my wasted life.
I hear once more the greetings of false friends
At Bacchic rite and orgiastic game;
Once more the frigid world my heart offends
With charges that I cannot now disclaim.
All round I hear foul slander's buzzing flight,
The judgments that the sly and stupid prate,
And envy's hiss, and pride's offended spite—
Malicious in its glee and bloody hate.
All joy has left me, and before my eyes
A pair of apparitions now appears:
Two cherished shades, two Angels from the skies,
Both sent to me by Fate in former years;
But each is winged—and bears a sword of flame
And guards me close—and ushers in my doom,
As both of them in deathly tones proclaim
The secrets of good fortune and the tomb.

These lines are actually a continuation of the poem on the preceding page. Pushkin, however, did not include the lines when he published the poem, perhaps due to the reference to the two women (probably Amalia Riznich and Countess Elizaveta Vorontsova). I have chosen, therefore, to print it separately here.

When she replaced, by some mistake,
With cordial *thou* the empty *you,*
I felt my throbbing heart awake
To sudden dreams of love anew;
And now I stand before this star
In pensive awe and cannot go;
I say aloud: how nice *you* are!
And think inside: I love *thee* so!

Written to Anna Olenina, to whom the poet proposed marriage in 1828; his suit
was rejected by her parents.

FRISKY FILLY

Don't be nervous, frisky bay,
You're of good Caucasian breed;
Don't go rushing off that way,
It's your time, my pretty steed;
Don't you squint that skittish eye,
Don't you paw and kick and rear,
Calm yourself and don't you fly
Off to meadows broad and clear.
Underneath my legs you'll learn
How to prance and how to turn;
I'll soon teach you to submit
When I jerk the bridle bit.

Another verse dedicated to Anna Olenina.

HER EYES
(A Reply to Some Lines by Prince Vyazemsky)

I quite agree—the lady's fair,
For courtiers an awesome prize,
And one might well indeed compare,
In verse, at least, to southern skies
Her luminous Circassian eyes.
How bold the glances they can send,
What fiery passions they implore.
But you'll agree I know, dear friend,
That my Olénin's eyes do more!
What pensive genius they express,
How sweet and innocent they seem,
What tenderness in their caress,
What liquid languor when they dream!
And when she shyly drops her gaze—
Her modest grace all else excels;
And when she lifts it—she displays
An angel face of Raphael's.

Pushkin's friend, Prince Peter Vyazemsky (1792–1878), a fellow poet and great wit, had written a poem ("Dark Eyes") to his and Pushkin's mutual acquaintance, Alexandra Smirnova-Rosset (1809–82). Pushkin responded with this tribute to Anna Olenina, whom he was courting.

Sing not, my love, sad Georgia's songs,
For they recall to me once more
A place for which the heart still longs,
Another life, a distant shore.

They call to mind with every tune—
Your melodies of mournful grace—
The steppe, and night, and by the moon
A faraway poor maiden's face.

And if I see you I forget
That fateful vision's sweet appeal;
But when you sing, it rises yet,
And all its haunting force I feel.

Sing not, my love, sad Georgia's songs,
For they recall to me once more
A place for which the heart still longs,
Another life, a distant shore.

Georgia (*Gruziya*), a province in southern Russia where Pushkin, during his exile, had reveled in the splendid scenery and in the happy adventurousness of his youth.

The "faraway poor maiden" is probably a reference to Maria Raevskaya-Volkonskaya (1805–63), a sister of the Raevsky brothers and one of Pushkin's early loves. She had followed her husband, Prince Sergey Volkonsky (1788–1865), to Siberia when he was exiled there for his involvement in the Decembrist uprising.

FOREBODING

Once again amid the stillness
Clouds have gathered round my head;
Jealous Fate prepares some illness,
Filling me once more with dread.
Shall I mock what Fate is sending?
Shall I meet it head unbowed,
Full of patience, but unbending,
As when I was young and proud?

Wearied by this helter-skelter,
Heedless of the storm I wait:
Maybe I shall find a shelter
From those heavy blows of Fate.
But I sense the dreaded Reaper,
As I hear the tolling bell;
Let me clasp you, Angel-Keeper,
By the hand to say farewell.

Gentle Angel, meek and mild,
Sadly murmur your good-byes;
Grieve for me, my tender child,
Raise or close your loving eyes;
All those thoughts of me you've cherished
Will sustain my soul instead,
Now that pride and strength have perished,
Now that youthful hopes have fled.

THE CONFIDANT

I grasp with greed each languid sigh,
Your heart's confessions, tender plaints;
How ravishing your ardent cry,
Those mad and frenzied sounds you make!
But halt this heavy recollection,
Conceal these dreams and do not moan:
I dread their feverish infection,
I dread to know what you have known!

OH BLEST IS HE WHOM YOU ADORE

Oh blest is he whom you adore,
The one to whom your passion bent,
Before whose eyes you melt and soar,
Whose glance commands your quick consent.

But wretched he who hangs his head,
Consumed by jealous love's distress,
Who hears in silence and with dread
When you his greatest fears confess.

19 OCTOBER 1828

Our prayers to God well made this day,
And having sung our lycée's cheers,
Farewell now, friends, I'm on my way,
And you should be in bed, my dears.

An anniversary poem for Pushkin's lycée schoolmates.

RAVENS

Raven to a raven flies,
Raven to a raven cries:
"Raven! Where shall we two eat?
Where shall we two find some meat?"

Raven answers raven so:
"There is food for us below:
By a willow on the plain
Lies a knight a foe hath slain."

By whose hand and why he fell
Only could his falcon tell,
And his mare of raven hue,
And his youthful widow, too.

Falcon to the grove did flit,
On the mare the foe did sit;
While the widow now doth wait
For a fresh and lively mate.

ANCHAR
(The Upas Tree)

Upon the barren desert sands,
On soil parched by summer's curse,
The Upas tree, dread sentry, stands—
Alone in all the universe.

There nature in the thirsty plain
One day in wrath brought forth the thing,
And to each root and leafy vein
It made a deadly poison cling.

The venom oozes down the bark,
Turned liquid by the blazing sun,
And then congeals amid the dark
Into a thick, transparent gum.

Upon that tree no bird will light,
No tiger come—the wind's black breath
Will circle round the tree of blight,
Then speed away, now laced with death.

And should a wayward cloud its dew
Upon those drooping leaves bestow,
The branches drip a fatal brew
Upon the burning sand below.

But once a man dispatched a man
With baleful look into that waste,
And he obeyed and off he ran
To bring the poison back in haste.

He brought the pitch upon a bough
Whose yellowed leaves had curled and died,
And on his pale and stricken brow
A chilling sweat poured down and dried.

And having brought it, he grew weak
And lay beneath the vaulted tent,
And at his mighty sovereign's feet
The wretched slave expired, spent.

And in that venomed sap the czar
Dipped arrows for his warrior bands
And sent destruction near and far
Upon the men of other lands.

A FLOWER

A scentless flower, pale and sere,
Forgotten in a book, I see;
And in my soul strange thoughts appear
That fill my mind with fancies free.

Where did it bloom? Some distant land?
Did it last long? Who plucked it then?
A stranger's or a lover's hand?
Why was it placed just here, and when?

In mem'ry of a tender talk?
Perhaps a fateful last farewell?
Picked on a silent, lonely walk
Through empty field and wooded dell?

Is he alive? Is she today?
In what far nook are those two hid?
Or have they both . . . faded away
As this forsaken flower did?

PORTENTS

I rode to you, and lively dreams
Swirled round about my giddy head;
And on my right the moonlight streamed
And followed closely where I led.

I rode away to other dreams;
My lovesick soul was now morose,
And on my left the moonlight streamed
And where I went it followed close.

We poets are condemned to dream
Amid the dark and stilly night,
And superstitious portents seem
To follow close and share our plight.

A RIDDLE
(On Sending a Bronze Sphinx)

Who in this snow planted seed from Theocritus' delicate
     roses?
Who in this iron age dreams of the great golden age of the
     Greeks?
Who is this mighty young Slav, this Teuton Hellenic in spirit?
Answer the riddle I pose, crafty old Oedipus, please!

This short verse was sent by Pushkin to his friend Delvig as a tribute.

Theocritus is an ancient Greek poet.

Upon the Georgian hills descends the mist of night;
    Aragva murmurs down below.
I feel both sad and calm; my grief itself is bright,
    This grief of you that fills me so—
Of you, of you alone—and nothing can undo
    Or overwhelm this sorrow's sway,
For thus my heart must burn and love—because it's true
    That not to love—it knows no way.

The Aragva is a river in Georgia.

AFTER HAFIZ
(A Camp on the Euphrates)

Don't be lured to martial glory,
O my young and handsome lord!
Don't rush off to battles gory,
Off to join the savage horde!
Yes, I know: you'll hardly perish;
Azrael, among the blades,
Will, I'm sure, your beauty cherish
And protect it from the shades!
Still, I fear: amid the battle
You will suffer all the same,
Lose your shy and modest manner,
Tender charm and sense of shame!

Hafiz, the fourteenth-century Persian poet.

Azrael, the angel of death in the Koran.

THAT CREVICE IN THE CLIFFSIDE HAZE
(A Fragment)

That crevice in the cliffside haze
Looms larger now and opens wide,
But calmer flows the Terek's tide,
The sun more brightly sheds its rays.

The Terek, a river in the Caucasus.

I RODE TO SOME FAR-DISTANT LAND

I rode to some far-distant land:
No rowdy feasts did I demand;
I sought not gold nor fame's reward
Amid the dust with lance and sword.

My soul I thirsted to restore
To live the life I lived before,
As in some sweet, forgetful haze
Beside the friends from bygone days.

I LOVED YOU ONCE

I loved you once—and love, it may well be,
Within my soul lies unextinguished yet.
But don't be troubled now by thoughts of me;
I wouldn't cause you sorrow or regret.

I loved you once—in silence and despair;
What jealous pangs, what timid fears I knew!
I loved you, though, with love so deep and rare,
As grant you God another's heart may do.

A final lyric addressed to Anna Olenina, who on the insistence of her parents, had rejected Pushkin's proposal of marriage. The poem has become famous in Russian.

A POOR AND SIMPLE KNIGHT

Long ago in some far region
Lived a poor and simple knight,
Pale and sorrowful of feature,
Yet in spirit full of might.

He had had a fateful vision,
Difficult to comprehend;
Deep within his heart implanted,
There it stayed, his only friend.

Once, when trav'ling to Geneva,
Neath a cross beside a spring,
He had seen the Virgin Mary,
Mother of the Christ, our King.

From that day, his soul ignited,
He on women looked no more
And until his dying moment
Speech with women he forswore.

From that day he never lifted
Metal visor from his face,
And instead of lady's favor
Wore a ros'ry in its place.

Never did our knight thereafter
Pray to Father or to Son
Or to Holy Ghost for succor;
Strange the life he'd now begun.

All night long for nights unending
He his mournful vigil kept;
Gazing sadly on the Virgin,
Streams of tears he softly wept.

Filled with faith and true devotion,
He to Heaven's Queen appealed,
Writing *Ave Mater Dei*
Bright with blood upon his shield.

As the knights on foaming horses
Flew across the valley plains,
Trembling Palestine could hear them
Calling out their ladies' names.

Lumen Coeli, Sancta Rosa!
Louder than the rest he cried,
Till the Muslim troops in panic
Fled the field on every side.

Home once more in distant castle,
He withdrew inside his gate,
Still in love and ever mournful,
Doomed to die inexpiate.

When the wretched knight lay dying,
To his couch a demon came,
Poised to seize his soul and take it
Deep within his dark domain.

He had failed to praise his Maker,
Never had he kept the fast;
He had shown the Holy Mother
Undue love until the last.

But our Lady, full of mercy,
Interceded for her knight
And admitted him forever
Into Heaven's deathless light.

When down the bustling streets I pass,
Or in a crowded church I stray,
Or share with frenzied youth a glass,
The same old thoughts assert their sway.

The years, I think, are rushing by,
And all our current merry band
Will one day in the graveyard lie,
And time for some is near at hand.

When on some lonely oak I gaze,
I muse on how that ancient wood
Will long outlive my sorry days,
As past our fathers' time it stood.

When I caress an infant's face,
I tell him in my mind: Farewell!
I yield to you this precious space;
My time to fade, and yours to swell.

I contemplate each passing year,
Each passing day, with bated breath
And wonder, as they disappear,
Which date will mark my coming death.

And where does Fate intend my end?
At sea—abroad—where battle reigns?
Or will some nearby valley lend
A plot to hold my mute remains?

Though senseless flesh will hardly care
Precisely where it goes to rot,
My final sleep I'd like to share
With some once well-belovèd spot.

And may young life in vigor play
Before that portaled tomb of mine
And heedless nature there, I pray,
In everlasting beauty shine.

ON SOME DRAWINGS FOR *EUGENE ONEGIN* IN THE *NEVSKY ALMANAC*

Just having crossed the Bridge Kokushkin,
His bottom to the rail applied,
Stands poet Alexander Pushkin,
Monsieur Onegin at his side.
Not deigning even once to peer
At fateful Power's Citadel,
He shows the place his haughty rear:
Don't spit, dear fellow, in the well.

One nipple shows through her chemise;
She's quite exposed—a charming sight!
She's crumpled paper on her knees;
Beset, alas, with stomach blight.
That's why she rose before the morn,
And why in moonlight's pallid beams,
To wipe herself Tatyana's torn
The *Nevsky Almanac,* it seems.

The indelicate mockery of these lines (which were, of course, not published) is directed at the illustrations to his verse novel that appeared in the above-mentioned journal. Onegin, Tatyana, and Pushkin himself are major characters in the novel.

THE COBBLER

A cobbler once perused a work of art
And noted that the shoes were wrongly drawn;
The artist then redid that tiny part.
The cobbler, arms akimbo, carried on:
"The face looks somewhat crooked to my eye—
And don't you think that bosom rather bare?"
To which Apelles promptly made reply:
"Confine yourself to shoes that people wear!"

Which brings to mind a fellow that I've met,
Whose field of expertise I now forget;
And though he feels compelled to share his views
On everything in life with no regret,
He, too, I think, should stick to judging shoes!

Apelles, celebrated Greek painter of the fourth century B.C., none of whose
works survive.

AT THE BUST OF A CONQUEROR

It's wrong to see a clumsy style:
The hand of art has truly wrought
Both marble lips that seem to smile
And brows that frown in angry thought.
This two-faced look he never shed,
For so he was, this potentate:
On inner conflicts he was fed,
A harlequin in face and fate.

The conqueror of the poem is Alexander I, the Czar who exiled Pushkin and whom he detested.

Lyrics

✦ 1830–1837 ✦

Verse written between 1830 and the poet's death in
1837, before he had completed his thirty-eighth year

CYCLOPS

I look at you with my one eye
And lose control of tongue and mind.
One eye is all my head contains;
But had it been the Fates' decree
That I should have a hundred eyes,
All hundred eyes would look at thee.

This verse was given to a lady friend of Pushkin's who was to attend a costumed
ball dressed as Cyclops and who wanted some verse to read before the Emperor
and Empress.

MY NAME

What does my name for you imply?
It's doomed to fade, to be no more:
A wave that breaks on a distant shore,
Off in the teeming night—a cry.

Soon it will leave its songs unsung,
These lifeless marks in an album placed:
Lines on a gravestone dimly traced
In some unfathomable tongue.

What's in it then? A time long dead
Of yearnings and their mad infection;
Upon your soul it will not shed
The tender rays of recollection.

But on some sad and silent day
Pronounce it with a sigh of pain,
And to a shadow's darkness say:
"There is one heart where I remain."

The poet inscribed this verse for the Polish beauty Karolina Sobanska, who had asked him to write his name in her memory album.

THE SONNET
(A Sonnet)

> *Scorn not the sonnet, critic.*
> Wordsworth

Unyielding Dante held the sonnet high;
Sweet Petrarch with his passion made it warm;
Macbeth's creator loved its playful eye;
Camoëns draped his sorrows with its form.
In our day, too, it's won the poets' praise:
The noble Wordsworth took it up in arms
When, far away from vain and worldly ways,
He drew us perfect nature and its charms;
And underneath Caucasia's distant skies,
The great Mickiéwicz heaved his mighty sighs
Within its close, encompassing embrace.
Our maidens, though, had not yet heard its strains
Till Délvig, too, abandoned for its grace
The sonorous hexameter's refrains.

Luis de Camoëns (1524–80), Portugal's national poet.

Adam Mickiewicz (1798–1855), Poland's national poet, whom Pushkin met and
befriended in Moscow in 1826. They spent time together later in St. Petersburg
and admired each other's poetry, although their differing political views kept
them from becoming close. Pushkin was as much an ardent Russian patriot as
Mickiewicz was a Polish nationalist, and they eventually clashed over Poland's
fight for independence.

TO THE POET

O poet! scorn the people's quick acclaim:
The moment of impassioned praise will cease,
The frigid crowd will laugh and fools defame,
But keep your firm resolve and be at peace.

Be czarlike—live alone and feel no shame.
Allow your inner freedom to increase;
Refine the fruits your cherished thoughts release,
Asserting for your noble deeds no claim.

For you alone must judge the work you do;
The strictest court of all resides in you.
And if you find it worthy, and your own?

Then let the motley crowd in fury curse
And spit upon the vessel of your verse
And try in puerile sport to shake your throne.

WHEN I CARESS YOU

When I caress you and adore
Your slender form in sweet embrace,
And filled with rapture I implore
With tender words your beauty's grace,
From my encircling arms you free
Your supple shape, and in reply
To my avowals all I see
Is your derisive, mocking eye;
Unsealing from your memory's store
The sad account of past deceits,
You listen but believe no more—
Unmoved and cold, your heart retreats.
I curse my mad, deluded fate,
My youthful craving for delight,
Those gardens where I used to wait
For secret trysts in dead of night;
I curse the lover's soft address,
The sweet, seductive song of verse,
The trustful maiden's soft caress,
Her tears and late regrets I curse.

Addressed to his wife, Natalya (Goncharova) Pushkina (1812–65).

VOLUPTUOUS DELIGHTS

Oh, no, I do not crave voluptuous delights,
Those ecstasies unbridled, those mad and frenzied rites,
Those ardent moans and cries a young Bacchante makes
When, snakelike in my arms, she writhes with lust and slakes
Her thirst with wounding bites, with hot, excited clasp,
And rushes to consume the shudder's final gasp!

How sweeter far are you, my gentle one, so shy!
What agonies of bliss when in your arms I lie,
And yielding to my long and ardent supplication,
You give yourself to me in tender resignation;
All cold and filled with shame, submissively you lie
And to my raptures give no welcoming reply.
Then slowly—more and more—you quicken to the beat:
Compelled to share at last my passion's flaming heat!

Addressed to his wife.

DEMONS

Clouds are racing, clouds are whirling;
Indistinct, the moon on high
Dimly lights the snow that's swirling
Through the murk of night and sky.
Over fields and meadows sweeping,
Sleigh bell tinkling—din, din, din—
Terror, terror, terror creeping
Through this endless land we're in!

"Forward, driver!"—"No way, Master,
Look: the horses struggle hard;
Flakes have sealed my eyes like plaster,
All the snowbound roads are barred:
I see nothing there to guide us,
Lost we are, with no way out!
Now some demon's come to ride us,
Dupe and drive us round about.

Look out there, out there: he's playing,
Hissing, spitting in my face;
Hear the frightened horses neighing
As toward the void they race.
Like some phantom signpost flashing,
Up ahead I see him loom;
There, just now, he sparkled, dashing
Through the vast and empty gloom."

Clouds are racing, clouds are whirling;
Indistinct, the moon on high
Dimly lights the snow that's swirling
Through the murk of night and sky.

We've no strength to go on racing:
Silent falls the tinkling bell.
Horses halt—"What's that we're facing?"—
"Wolf or tree stump, who can tell?"

Raging still, the storm advances;
Nervous horses snort and turn;
Far ahead the demon dances,
Just his eyes in darkness burn.
Once again the sleigh goes fleeting,
Tinkling bell goes—din, din, din—
Now I see the specters meeting
Mid this white expanse we're in.

Endless, monstrous faces sputter
Through the murky moonlit night;
Hosts of demons flit and flutter
Like November leaves in flight,
Hordes of them that wail and scurry.
Why their plaintive, dirgelike lay?
Have they come some beast to bury?
For some witch's wedding day?

Clouds are racing, clouds are whirling;
Indistinct, the moon on high
Dimly lights the snow that's swirling
Through the murk of night and sky.
Demons swarm on swarm come sailing
Through the vast, unending spheres,
As their mournful shrieks and wailing
Rend my heart with nameless fears.

ELEGY

The frenzied joys of youth have turned to waste,
Their residue a harsh and bitter taste;
And in my soul the sorrows of the past,
Like wine, take on with age a stronger cast.
My path is dark: the stormy seas ahead
Now promise me great labor, woe, and dread.

But, O my friends, I want no deathly fate;
I yearn to live, to suffer and create.
I know there will be joys and exaltations
Amid the sorrows, cares, and tribulations;
That once again sweet harmony I'll find,
That tears of inspiration will be mine;
And, maybe, in the sunset of my day
Bright love will cast a parting smile my way.

THE PAGE, OR AT AGE FIFTEEN

C'est l'âge de Chérubin

My fifteenth year will soon arrive;
I long to see the joyous day,
For when it comes I'll truly thrive!
Yet even now no man alive
Would cast a mocking glance my way.

I'm not a boy—I twirl the hair
Upon my upper lip, you see;
I sport an elder's knowing air
And gravel voice, as you're aware—
So watch your step when you're with me.

The ladies like my modest ways,
And one among them steals my breath—
She wields a haughty, languid gaze
And on her cheek such blushes blaze
That I for her would suffer death.

She's so majestic and so bold,
She has the most amazing mind—
And jealous! You should see her scold!
But though you'd find her proud and cold,
Alone with me she's warm and kind.

She swore with regal wrath last night
That if I ever dared again
To cast my eye to left or right,
She'd give me poison at the sight—
For that's how much she loves her men!

She's ready, scorning worldly shame,
To fly with me to desert cell.
You'd like to know the lady's name?
My countess from the south of Spain?
Oh, no, I swear, I'll never tell.

A YOUTH

Close by the bitter, cold sea, a fisherman hoisted his net.
There at his side was his son. Leave him, my boy, when
  you can!
Duties far greater await you—nets of a kind never seen:
You'll be a counsel to kings; you'll be a fisher of men.

The youth to which the poem refers is Mikhail Lomonosov (1711–65), eminent
eighteenth-century scientist and man of letters. The son of a peasant fisherman,
he ran away from home at the age of seventeen and eventually had an illustrious
career. He was largely responsible for the founding of Moscow University.

NO CYPRIAN ROSES

No Cyprian roses,
Dew-dappled and fine,
In song do I greet;
No scolion roses,
All sprinkled with wine,
In verse do I treat;
But roses that faded
With joy on the breast
Of Liza, my sweet . . .

Cyprian roses, roses of Aphrodite.

Scolion, a song sung at banquets in ancient Greece.

BOUND FOR YOUR HOMELAND FAR AWAY

Bound for your homeland far away,
You bade a foreign land good-bye;
That dismal, unforgotten day—
How long before you then I cried.
My hands grew cold, but sought to make
You linger there for yet a spell;
My cry implored you not to break
The awful anguish of farewell.

But from that bitter, bitter kiss
You tore away at last your face;
Across a bleak and sharp abyss
You called me to another place.
You said: "When once again we meet,
Where skies are always blue above,
Beneath the shade of olive trees
We'll taste again the kiss of love."

But there, alas, where arching skies
Forever sparkle blue and deep,
Where olive shade on water lies,
You're sleeping now the final sleep.
Your beauty, suffering, and bliss
Have disappeared along with you
And with them now our promised kiss—
But still I wait; it still is due.

Written in memory of Amalia Riznich.

GYPSIES
(From the English)

High above the wooded banks,
Late at night, amid the still,
Sighs and singing fill their ranks,
Scattered fires dot the hill.

Hail to you, you happy tribe!
I have known your camps before;
I myself in other times
Might have shared your tented shore.

Come the dawn, you'll drift away,
Leave no trace upon that shore;
You'll depart—your poet stay,
Freedom's path is his no more.

He's abandoned nomad nights,
All the mischief, all the grief,
Turned his eye to homely sights,
Quiet hearth and country peace.

ECHO

When beast in darkest forest roars,
When trumpet brays or thunder pours,
When maidens sing on distant shores—
    To each of these
Through vacant air your echo soars
    In quick reprise.

You heed the rumbling thunder's knell,
The voice of storm and ocean swell,
The call of rustic shepherd's bell—
    And send reply,
But nothing echoes through the dell
    The poet's cry!

TO A BOY
(After Catullus)

Minister vetuli, puer

Fill the cup, my boy, with wine,
Strong Falernus wine with bite:
So Postumia commands,
Mistress of our Bacchic rite.
You, you waters, flow away;
With your stream that weakens wine
Succor those who now abstain;
Only Bacchus here must reign.

Falernus (or Falernian) wine, a type of wine much celebrated by Latin poets.

Surrounded by the motley crew
That crowds the court on every side,
I kept intact a frigid view,
A simple heart and open mind;
I nursed the noble flame of truth,
And like a child I was kind.
I mocked the crowd and all its ways,
Made judgments that were sane and bright,
And filled my album's every page
With epigrams of blackest spite.

Pushkin inscribed this verse in an album that he presented to his friend, Alexandra Smirnova-Rosset. She was close to the royal family, and Pushkin asked her to write in the album her observations of life at court.

ON A YOUNG LADY

I must not, cannot, do not dare
Insanely yield to passion's pains;
I guard my inner calm with care
And keep my sober heart in chains;
Enough of love; but am I free
To dream a passing dream at times,
When accidentally I see
A pure, angelic girl go by
And disappear? And may I then,
Admiring her with longing gaze,
Pursue her with my eyes and send
My blessings on her carefree days,
And wish her peacefulness of heart
And all the deepest joys of life—
Yes, even happiness for him
Who makes the charming girl his wife.

The verse refers to Countess Nadezhda Sologub (1815–1903), a young lady
whose beauty attracted both Pushkin's eye and his wife's jealousy.

The mighty festive god of grapes
Allows us each to drink in toast
Three glasses at the evening feast.
The first one in the Graces' name,
Those naked beauties clothed in shame;
The second glass we dedicate
To rosy-cheeked good health and cheer;
The third to long-lived friendship's bonds;
But when the third has disappeared,
The wiser heads lay down their wreaths
And sing their most effusive song
To bléssèd Morpheus in sleep.

FEAST WITH RESTRAINT

Celebrant, feast with restraint!
Mix with the liquor of Bacchus
Water's good sobering stream,
And sage conversation as well.

WINE
(Ion of Chios)

Rowdy in youth and youthful in age,
A good-natured sovereign lord,
Filling our hearts with ardor and pride,
Patron of revels and love!

Ion of Chios, Greek poet of the fifth century B.C., from the island of Chios.

MAECENAS
(After Horace)

Maecenas, heir to mighty kings,
O ancient patron of the arts!
Some send their chariots on wings
Of golden dust to stable yards;
And when their flaming wheels have reached
The safety of their walled estate,
They think they've earned a victory wreath
And call themselves the gods of fate.
Still others gather to their brows
Great rank and titles of repute;
Quirites of the fickle crowd
Defer to them—and some salute.

Quirites, citizens of ancient Rome.

On the open fields and spaces
Snow is glist'ning silver bright;
Neath the moon my troika races
Down the highway through the night.

Sing when boredom sets you drowsing,
When the road is dark and long;
Oh, how sweet I find the rousing
Sounds of native Russian song!

Driver, sing! And do it boldly:
Let me hear those old refrains.
Look, the moon now glitters coldly,
While the mournful wind complains.

Sing the song "O little torch,
Won't you burn more brightly still?"

The last two lines do not rhyme in the Russian.

Did not some vague ambition's blight
Confound my soul, I know not why,
I'd stay right here and sip delight
Beneath this dim and distant sky:
I'd let all trembling wishes go,
I'd call the world an idle show—
That I forever might, my sweet,
Attend your lips and kiss your feet.

Why is it that she charms me so?
Why is it she and I must part?
If only I could overthrow
The habits of my gypsy heart . . .

. . . .

She always looks at you so sweetly,
Her chatter captivates completely,
Her spirits always seem so high,
Her lovely eyes so warm and shining.
And then last night, as we were dining,
Beneath the table, on the sly,
She rubbed her foot against my thigh!

VARIANT

She looks at you with tender passion,
She chatters in such careless fashion,
Her subtle mirth is meant to tease,
Her lovely eyes so warm and shining.
And then last night as we were dining,
Beneath the table with such ease
She slid her foot between my knees!

AUTUMN
(A Fragment)

What doesn't enter then my drowsy mind?
Derzhavin

I

October has arrived—and now the grove
Has shed its final leaves from naked boughs;
The autumn cold has blown—and frozen roads.
Behind the mill the burbling brook still sounds;
But now the pond is still. My neighbor goes
Off to the distant fields to hunt. His hounds
Will wake the woods with all their barking noise,
As winter wheat is crushed by frenzied joys.

II

This is my time! For spring I do not pine;
I'm bored with nature's thaw—the stink and mud.
Spring makes me ill and fills my soul and mind
With too-discordant dreams and stirs my blood.
But winter's stern demeanor suits me fine:
The moonlit snow when, in a sleigh, your love,
All warm and eager underneath the furs,
Will squeeze your hand with trembling touch of hers.

III

What joy to glide, with feet in iron skates,
Across the mirror of the river's trace!
And what of sparkling winter's holy dates?

But still—one must admit it's hard to face
Six months of snow. The bear himself must hate
So long a sojourn in a cooped-up place.
And even sleighing with young beauties palls,
Or stewing by the stove inside your walls.

IV

O wondrous Summer! I would hold you dear,
If heat and dust and gnats and flies were out!
They dull our faculties and smother cheer;
And we, like meadows, suffer from the drought.
Our one escape is drinking wine or beer—
There's nothing else to do but dream about
Old Mother Winter and her farewell feast,
So we salute her—with ice-cream at least.

V

Men often curse chill autumn's final days,
But I, dear reader, always see with love
Her gentle beauty, with its somber blaze.
She touches me the way a child does,
For whom none cares. And frankly I must say,
That fall's the only time of year I love;
She's kind and good; and in her I discover
A wayward dream to charm a humble lover.

VI

But how can I explain this love of mine?
Perhaps you've felt a fondness of your own
For some consumptive girl condemned to die,
Who suffers without anger or a moan.

Upon her pallid lips one sees a smile;
The yawning grave to her is yet unknown;
Upon her face still plays a crimson glow;
She's still alive today, tomorrow no.

VII

O time of sorrow that enchants the gaze!
The beauty of your parting fills my soul—
I love the splendid fading of those days,
The forest clothed in crimson and in gold,
The rustling leaves, the heavens' shimmered haze,
The freshness of the air and hint of cold,
The thinning rays of sun, an early freeze,
The threat of hoary winter in the breeze.

VIII

Whenever autumn comes I bloom serene;
For me the Russian cold's a healthy treat
And once again I relish life's routine:
I sleep a lot and sometimes even eat;
The blood within my heart flows quick and keen;
I'm young again and glad with passion's heat
And full of life once more—for so I'm made
(Permit me this prosaic turn of phrase).

IX

They lead my stallion up and, mane unfurled,
He gallops down the meadow's frozen ground;
And as he bears his rider through the world,
Beneath his hoofs the cracking ice resounds.

But soon the daylight dims, and then I'm curled
Before the hearth to read some book I've found
Or nourish in my soul expansive dreams,
While now and then the ebbing flame still gleams.

X

The world forgot—amid the dulcet night
I yield once more to sweet imagination,
And once again poetic thought takes flight.
The soul, undone by lyric agitation,
Convulses—cries—and in a flood of light,
Brings forth at last the fruit of free creation:
And I am then the host of guests unseen,
Long known to me, the harvest of my dreams.

XI

And now my head is filled with bold conceits,
And in a rush to meet them races *Rhyme*,
And fingers seek the pen, and pen—the sheets;
One moment—and the verses flow in time!
Just so a moveless ship on moveless seas
Is lost in sleep. But look! The seamen climb
The rigging—and the sails, inflated, sweep;
The great ship moves—and cleaves the salty deep.

XII

It sails. But whither is it bound?

GOD GRANT THAT I NOT GO INSANE

God grant that I not go insane.
Far better were a sack and cane,
Harsh labor or a pauper's share.
It isn't that I hold my mind
In such esteem, nor would I find
The parting from it hard to bear.

Were I but left alone and free,
How gladly and how quick I'd flee
To where the wooded darkness teems.
In flaming frenzy would I sing
And in a mindless stupor cling
To wondrous and discordant dreams.

I'd harken to the pounding waves,
And, filled with ecstasy, I'd gaze
Through all the vast and vacant skies.
A free and mighty force I'd stand
And, like a whirlwind, rout the land
And ravage all the forest wide.

But here's the rub: go mad and see
How dreaded as the plague you'll be;
They'll pen you up with no release,
They'll chain you to a madman's fate;
And men will come and through the grate
They'll taunt you like a wretched beast.

And in the darkness I shall hear
No songbird's voice serene and clear,
No rustling murmur of the oak—

But my companions' cries of fright,
The cursing of the watch at night,
The shrieks, the clanking of the yoke.

IT'S TIME, MY FRIEND, IT'S TIME

It's time, my friend, it's time! My spirit yearns for peace.
As day succeeds on day, each moment we release
Some particle of life; and though both you and I
Are hungering to live, tomorrow we may die.
There is no joy on earth, but peace and freedom wait:
Long since I've had a dream of some far-better fate;
Long since—a weary slave—I've dreamt of taking flight
To some far-distant land of work and pure delight.

Probably addressed to his wife.

THOSE DAYS OF STORM

I've persevered amid the tempest's blast,
And now the turbid current of my life
Has found a quiet haven from the past,
Reflecting in its depths the azure sky.

But will it stay? I'd like to think they're gone,
Those days of storm, of dark and bitter longing.

I stand among the graves and mourn;
I look about and think of ends.
The sacred ashes lie forlorn,
And all around the steppe extends.
A country lane lies near at hand,
And now and then I hear the sound
Of wagon wheels against the sand
As they go past the hallowed ground.
Bare fields are all the eye can see,
No brook, no hill, no lonely tree.
Among the graves and silent stones
A few scant bushes dot the land,
And wooden crosses, row on row,
Monotonous and mournful stand.

ODE LVI
(From Anacreon)

Now my hair has thinned and grayed,
Curls that once I wore with pride;
Teeth as well have now decayed,
Sparkles in my eyes have died.
All life's sweetness has to fade,
Few the days that still remain;
Fate's account must soon be paid,
Hades beckons down the lane.
We'll not rise from out those walls,
There for good the curtain falls:
There the yawning doorway gapes—
All will enter, none escapes.

ODE LVII
(From Anacreon)

Look, we've let the cup go dry!
Come, my lad, and pour me more;
But dilute the drunken wine,
Sober water also pour.
We're not Mongols—I dislike
Drunken orgies, friends, I swear:
No, I sing when drinking wine
Or in harmless talk I share.

AFTER ANDRÉ CHÉNIER

The cloak, well-fortified and soaked with bitter blood,
The Centaur's vengeful gift as pledge from jealous love,
To Hercules was borne. Which Hercules embraced.
Inside those noble veins the potent poison raced;
And now his martyred rage, abroad at midnight, howls;
Across the holy mount with heavy tread he prowls:
He breaks and shatters trees; uprooted trunks he heaps
To make a mighty mound; and now the madman leaps
To light the massive pyre. He steps inside the blaze
And, lying down to wait, on Heaven turns his gaze.
His club was at his side, his lion trophy, too,
Lay spread across his feet; the wind, with shrieking, blew;
The flames were crackling high, and, roaring as they swelled,
They lofted to the sky the deathless soul they held.

Just last night my Lila sweet
Rose to make a quick retreat.
When I asked her: "Won't you stay?"
Her reply was indiscreet:
"All your hair has turned to gray."
Then I told the saucy miss:
"Everything must fade one day!
That which once was musky bliss
Reeks of camphor now, I'd say."
On these sorry words I said,
Lila's laughing answer fell:
"You yourself must know full well—
Sweet is musk for newlywed,
Camphor masks the coffin's smell."

ARABIC IMITATION

Tender youth and lover tender,
Mine forever, have no shame;
Rebels both, we won't surrender,
Life has made us both the same.
I don't mind the constant mocking:
Two can bear it twice as well;
We're twin walnuts interlocking,
Wrapped inside a single shell.

I do not greatly prize those ringing "rights"
That drive so many minds to giddy heights.
I mutter no complaint that God is lax
In letting me dispute a heavy tax
Or hinder kings from warring on their kind;
Nor care I if the Press is free to blind
The witless, or if censors can abuse
Some scribbler's clever efforts to amuse.
All these are only *words, words, words,* you see;
For other, higher rights are dear to me;
And other, higher freedoms do I sing:
Dependence on the people or the king—
What difference does it make? Abandon these!
To give account to none, to serve and please
Oneself alone; and not to bow in fright
One's conscience, thought or head—to rank and might;
To wander where one will as fancy drifts,
Profoundly moved by nature's godlike gifts,
All tremulous in joyous exaltation
Before the works of art and inspiration—
My happiness is this and these are rights.

Ippolyte Pindemonte (1753–1828), Italian poet. Despite its title, this poem is actually an original work of Pushkin's; he labeled it a translation out of concern for the censor.

SECULAR POWER

Upon that day of triumph and of loss,
When torment took our Lord upon the Cross,
Beneath the Tree of Life, on either side,
Immersed in overwhelming sorrow's tide,
Two pale and stricken women could be seen:
The Holy Virgin and the Magdalene.
But now beneath the Sacred Cross we see,
In place of those poor women by the tree,
Two armed and visored sentries grimly wait,
As if to guard the city ruler's gate.
But what's the purpose, keeper, of your task?
Or is the Cross state baggage, may I ask,
To be secured from mice or thieving horde?
Or would you thus add glory to the Lord?
What grace could all your worldly power bring
To One whose crown of thorns has made him King,
The Christ who gave His body to the flails,
Who humbly bore the lance and piercing nails?
Or do you fear the rabble might disgrace
The One whose death redeemed the human race;
And so, to guard the strolling gentry's way,
You bar and keep the common folk at bay?

In vain I seek to flee to Zion's holy mount;
No matter where I turn, my sins will sniff me out—
For so the hungry beast thrusts nostrils in the ground
To track the pungent path the fleeing deer laid down.

A PRAYER

Our hermit monks and women pure as snow,
In order to transcend this world below,
To steel the heart against its storm and strife,
Have offered many prayers to hallow life;
But none of them has proved to me more dear
Than one the priest recites at Lent each year;
It rises to my lips those days of grief
And offers to this sinner sweet relief:

"Come purge my soul, Thou Master of my days,
Of vain and empty words, of idle ways,
Of base ambition and the urge to rule,
That hidden serpent that corrupts a fool;
And grant me, Lord, to see my sins alone.
That I not call my brother to atone;
Make chaste my heart and lend me from above
Thy fortitude, humility, and love."

When, lost in thought, beyond the town I stray
And come upon a graveyard on my way,
Where railings, pillars, and the polished stones
Conceal the city's dead and rotting bones,
All packed within the swamp, a jumbled horde,
Like greedy guests that crowd a beggar's board;
Where tombs of merchants and officials stand,
The graceless work of some cheap mason's hand,
Whose verse and prose inscriptions offer thanks
For all their virtues, services, and ranks;
And cuckold's tomb, adorned with widow's grief,
The columns shorn of vases by some thief;
And slimy graves awaiting with a yawn
Arrival of their tenants in the dawn—
Oh, all of this conveys so bleak an air
And fills me with such deep and foul despair,
I'd like to spit and flee—

                And yet I love,
On autumn eves, when silence reigns above,
To visit some ancestral village keep,
Where all the dead in solemn stillness sleep;
Where every simple marker has a home,
And in the dark no pallid robbers roam;
Where only some old villager comes by
To greet the mossy stones with prayer and sigh.
In place of petty pyramids and vases,
Of noseless Angels and disheveled Graces,
A spreading oak looms high above the graves
And, rustling, stirs . . .

OH, NO, I DO NOT FIND LIFE OLD

Oh, no, I do not find life old,
I love it and would yet live on;
My soul with time has not grown cold,
Although its youthful bloom is gone.
There still remain those keen delights
Of curiosity of mind,
Of inspiration's happy flights,
Of feelings—and of life.

I THOUGHT MY HEART HAD LEARNED

I thought my heart had learned to shun
That anguish it so often bore;
I told myself that dreams undone
Would be no more, would be no more!
That joy was gone and grief as well,
And all illusion put to rest—
But now once more they pulse and swell
At sovran beauty's dread behest.

MONUMENT

Exegi monumentum

A monument I've raised—not built by human hand.
The people's path to it will not be overgrown;
Its splendid head unbowed, more lofty does it stand
    Than Alexander's mighty stone.

Not all of me will die, for through my art, I know,
My soul shall long outlive my mortal body's death,
And I shall be renowned while on this earth below
    At least one poet still draws breath.

And word of me shall spread through all the lands of *Rus*
And all her many tribes shall proudly speak my name:
The haughty Slav, the Finn, the yet untamed Tungus,
    The Kalmuk of the distant plain.

And I shall be revered by peoples near and far—
That in my hallowed verse I summoned kindly thought,
That in this savage age I sang of Freedom's star
    And mercy for the fallen sought.

Be ever faithful, Muse, and honor God's command;
To praise and slander both—be reticent and cool;
Of insult have no fear, no laurel wreath demand,
    And never argue with a fool.

The Latin epigraph ("I raised a monument") quotes the opening words of
an ode by Horace, and the poem as a whole is a variation on Horace's ode.
Pushkin's great predecessor Gavriil Derzhavin (1743–1816) had provided him

with a model in his own fine variation on Horace's ode. "Alexander's mighty stone" refers to the granite column that was erected on the Palace Square in 1834 in memory of Czar Alexander I. Pushkin intentionally absented himself from St. Petersburg on the day of its dedication.

Rus, an ancient and poetic name for Russia.